"Scott McNamara is a gifted evangelist with personal experience of the Holy Spirit changing lives today."

Nicky Gumbel, pioneer, Alpha; vicar, HTB, London

"We've been hugely inspired and en~~ ~~ ~~ ~~ v Scott and his ministry. His pass~~ ~~ ~~ ~~ ~~ ~~ ~~ ~~ ~~ ~~ e lost is infectious and has left ~~ ~~ ~~ ~~ ~~ ~~ ~~ ~~ ~~ ~~ treet

"The principles in this book ~~ ~~ ~~ ~~ onized my life as a Catholic. When Scott shared them with me, they lit a fire under me to start sharing the Gospel the way I always wanted to but never knew how. This book is going to challenge, encourage and equip you to do what Jesus told us to do."

Fr. Columba Jordan, CFR, Catholic priest and member of the
Community of the Franciscan Friars of the Renewal

"*Jesus at the Door* is the most effective evangelism tool I have ever come across and personally used. This guide will not only take you wonderfully through the nine step Jesus at the Door process but also give you a fiery passion to reach the lost and partner with God to see lives transformed by the Gospel!"

Reuben Morley, Billy Graham Evangelistic Association

"I've been encouraged in every encounter I've had with Scott. He's a relentlessly positive, joyful evangelist that practices what he preaches every single day. So many of us struggle in sharing our faith. We need simple, powerful tools to help us experience the joy of seeing people respond to the Good News. Do we believe God can and will use us, as we obey? That the Holy Spirit is going before us every day? That evangelism is joining the Holy Spirit in a conversation he's already having with someone? Read *Jesus at the Door* and get ready for the journey of a lifetime."

Kevin Palau, president, Luis Palau Association

"Scott has an incredible gift, the very rare combination of a five-fold evangelist and teacher. *Jesus at the Door* breathes the very heart of God to our world at this time. It empowers and equips believers in a way that I've never seen before. I recommend this to every Christian."

Roger Pearce, apostolic leader, Every Nation Southern Africa

"Scott and Jaye McNamara are going to change the world with Jesus at the Door. I have seen it firsthand out on the streets and even at Korn's concerts. God's presence is in this ministry in a very unique way. I can honestly say I have not seen the dramatic after-effects with follow-up and discipleship in other ministries like I have seen with Jesus at the Door."

Brian "Head" Welch, co-founder of the Grammy Award–winning band Korn; *New York Times* bestselling author, *Save Me from Myself*; co-star, *Loud Krazy Love*

"Scott McNamara is a firebrand of the faith. His passion for evangelism and insights into reaching the lost have inspired and enriched us. His Jesus at the Door model has been a blessing to our church, helping many of us get out of our comfort zones and share the Gospel."

John and Debby Wright, senior pastors, Trent Vineyard, Nottingham, England; national directors, Vineyard Churches UK and Ireland

JESUS

AT THE

DOOR

JESUS

AT THE

DOOR

EVANGELISM MADE EASY

SCOTT McNAMARA

Chosen

a division of Baker Publishing Group
Minneapolis, Minnesota

Published by Chosen Books
11400 Hampshire Avenue South
Minneapolis, Minnesota 55438
www.chosenbooks.com

Chosen Books is a division of
Baker Publishing Group, Grand Rapids, Michigan

Printed in the United States of America

ISBN 978-0-8007-6191-2

Library of Congress Control Number: 2020943524

Many names and other identifying characteristics of individuals in this book have been changed to protect their privacy.

Cover design by Studio Gearbox

Baker Publishing Group publications use paper produced from sustainable forestry practices and post-consumer waste whenever possible.

Holy Spirit,

Thank you for schooling me and showing me firsthand
what evangelism really is. Thank you for allowing me
to partner with you and for giving me a front-row seat
on a daily basis to watch you, the star of the show,
do what only you can do—reveal Jesus.

Make me a neon sign that points to you.
Let them see me shine just long enough to point them to you.

CONTENTS

FOREWORD

BY DANIEL KOLENDA

AT OUR MINISTRY headquarters in Orlando, we have a huge picture of one of our mass Gospel campaigns in Africa. The picture is so large it covers the entire wall from one end to another and from floor to ceiling, up a flight of stairs to the second level. Once during a School of Evangelism, an evangelist was standing there for fifteen or twenty minutes, just staring. Finally, someone asked him if he was all right, and his answer is something I will never forget. "I've just been trying to figure out how to get from here to there," he said as he pointed to the picture.

I have found that this is one of the most common felt needs in the Body of Christ, particularly in the area of evangelism. People want to make a difference. They want to win the lost. They want to lead people to Jesus. But how? It's often not the inspiration or passion that is missing, but the practical tools. Many books and seminars on evangelism specialize in the inspirational but lack the hands-on, concrete instruction that people so badly need.

In Ephesians 4:11–12, where Scripture lists the five-fold ministry offices, it says that their function is "to *equip the saints* for the work of ministry" (emphasis added). We need evangelists, not only for evangelism, but to equip the Body of Christ for evangelism.

Right now, I believe we are entering what will be known as the greatest era for evangelism in Church history. All over the world, I have seen a surge of interest in the Body of Christ to win the lost. I'm not just talking about professional career preachers. I'm not just talking about people who preach (or want to preach) in stadiums. I'm talking about ordinary believers who want to share Jesus with their friends, their family, their co-workers and their neighbors. Moreover, they have a great desire, not only to share the Gospel, but to do it with power. They want to see people's lives transformed through an encounter with Jesus.

Without question, the hunger is there. I have seen it with my own eyes all over the globe. But God's people need to be equipped with the tools to do the job. Even as you read these words right now, you might be thinking, *I want to win souls, but how? How do I get from where I am today to where I want to be?*

This is why I am so thankful for Scott McNamara's *Jesus at the Door*. He has given us a tool that I believe will result in multitudes of salvations. He has demystified the often dreaded work of evangelism, making it easy, simple and powerful. Once you see how effective you can be in winning souls, you will be hooked!

Also, for those who might need inspiration, Scott has an infectious way of imparting his passion for souls to the reader. It's not just head-to-head information, it's a heart-to-heart impartation. I am confident that this book will equip you for evangelism in every way.

Daniel Kolenda, president and CEO,
Christ For All Nations

ACKNOWLEDGMENTS

MY PRECIOUS MUM, Sheila McNamara, you faithfully prayed me into the Kingdom. You always believed that God could and would do something with a man like me, despite how I looked to the rest of the world. You live a selfless life and are the kind of hero heaven celebrates. I'm honored to be your son.

My sister Amy-Joy, you're a gift from heaven. The Lord used your life to change mine. I love you, sweets.

Jaye McNamara, you showed me Christlike love and forgiveness in my darkest hour, and without your love, I wouldn't be here today. I'm everything I am because you loved me.

This book wouldn't have been possible if not for the patience and support shown by my beloved wife, Jaye, and kids, Sienna, Ruby, Elijah and Martha. Thank you all for being patient with me while I was locked away in my room writing this book.

Promise Church, thank you for opening your hearts to my family and me, showing us what the greatest church in the world looks like.

Thank you to Chosen Books and especially Jane Campbell for not only being willing to believe in what the Lord has given me in Jesus at the Door, but also being there to council me through the process of writing my first book.

Alan Scott, thank you for having the vision and enough faith in what the Lord had placed on my life to employ me as a full-time evangelist, and for giving me room to grow into all that the Father had ordained me to be.

Robby Dawkins, thanks not only for believing in me enough to connect me with Chosen Books, but for championing me and other evangelists you see the Lord's hand on, and ensuring their gifts rise to the surface in order to bless the Body of Christ.

Christopher "I've got hold of the truth and I feel dangerous" William Lockwood—thanks for praying for me for all those years, and then when your prayers were answered, for discipling me. You're a radical John the Baptist–type disciple, and what you invested in me in those formative years I live out today. You can be my wingman anytime.

Thank you, Daniel Kolenda, for writing the foreword for this book. It is an honor to know you. Your heart of humility and purity exudes Jesus.

Dave Orange, an unsung hero of the faith and heaven's secret weapon. You inspire me to be more like Jesus. It is because of you and your family that I am on this journey. #AllforJesus

ONE

GOD WANTS REAPERS

LET ME BE clear from the outset—I am not trying to guilt you into feeling worse about evangelism than you already do. Instead, this book will show you how you—yes, even you—can move from being a seasoned sower into a relentless reaper, living out a naturally supernatural lifestyle, partnering with the Holy Spirit in the harvest fields of life to bring glory to the Father as you bear much fruit (see John 15:8).

I am going to teach you how to use what I call "reaping style" evangelism. Bono from U2 describes beautifully and exactly what reaping style evangelism is in this advice he received once from a pastor: "Stop asking God to bless what you are doing. Find out what God's doing. It is already blessed."

Jesus at the Door is what I call a reaping tool because it does this very thing. It focuses so closely on partnership with the Spirit that we go only where He is going. If we do that, then the worst thing that will happen is that we will sow.

Nine Points and a Picture

Jesus at the Door is framed around a card with nine prompts and a picture to help guide you in a conversation with unbelievers. I call this our Equipping Card, and one is included for you in this book. Here I will give the framework to help you understand what I am talking about when I mention the picture or card, and the next nine chapters will expand on each of the nine points so you will have confidence to use them. That means you can relax. You can flip back and forth between the card and the descriptions any time you want to, so there is no need to worry, get bogged down in details or feel that you have to memorize this.

First, Jesus at the Door begins with a picture. It is a very simple, but powerful and anointed picture. It shows Jesus knocking on a door with no outer doorknob. In other words, He cannot let Himself in; we have to let Him in. Jesus and the door are framed by a heart, so very quickly, at a glance, any person can see that Jesus is knocking on the door of his or her heart wanting to come in.

Next, as you share the Gospel, you simply guide your conversation through these nine prompts.

1. Have you seen this picture before, and do you pray? (In emergencies? Do you believe God is there?)
2. This is Jesus knocking on the door of your heart, but the handle is on the inside. Only you can let Him in.
3. Lots of people pray . . . but praying is like talking through the door: You know He is there somewhere, but you don't know Him personally.
4. Visualize wearing a backpack. If we filled it with all your sin, would it be heavy? That represents your debt with God. It stops you from having a relationship with Him.

5. If you owed the bank $10,000, and I gave you a check for that amount, and you deposited it into your account, what would happen to your debt?

6. That's what Jesus did for you on the cross. He wrote you a check signed in His blood. Today He is standing at the door of your heart, wanting you to cash it.

7. If Jesus were here right now, would you let Him in?

8. Can you see the wind? No, but you can feel it, right? Like the wind, Jesus is here right now. May I pray for you to feel His presence?

9. Now for the last thing: to turn from the road you're on without Jesus, change direction and follow Him. Do you want to follow Him?

The first three pertain to the picture and have a blue background. The next three symbolize sin and have a red background. And the final three reveal repentance and have a yellow background. At the bottom of the card is a prayer to lead them to Jesus right then and there.

There is nothing fancy about this method. It simply puts forth the Gospel plain and simple. I felt the Lord highlight 1 Corinthians 2:13 as a passage that best defines what Jesus at the Door really is: "When we tell you these things, we do not use words that come from human wisdom. Instead, we speak words given to us by the Spirit, using the Spirit's words to explain spiritual truths."

Out in the Deep

I remember the day my pastor, Alan Scott, called me, excited to tell me the good news that he was offering me a job as a full-time evangelist, working for Causeway Coast Vineyard Church. I was in the middle of leading a guy to the Lord in a café. I mean, literally, he was repeating the prayer with me and I had to silence my phone as it rang mid-prayer. You could not have planned it if you had tried. Alan posted on social media later that day: "I called my friend to offer him a job as an evangelist. He couldn't take the call, as he was leading someone to Jesus. I think we got the right guy!"

I think it was the Lord encouraging us both that we were making the right decision.

My job would be to stand on the streets all day every day, let down my nets and catch. It would be an understatement to say I felt out of my depth. In their fifteen-year history they had never employed an evangelist, and I had never been one, so it was a leap of faith on both parts. It was made only the more tenuous by my pastor's comments that this job was a six-month trial position that was dependent on fruit—his desire was for me to lead one soul a day to Jesus.

I would have called myself more of a sowing evangelist up until that point. I was leading someone to the Lord on average once every five weeks. I did not really know what I was doing, however, and walked away from the majority of those encounters at that time thinking, *I should have said this*, or *I should have done that.*

So when I stepped out onto those streets as a full-time evangelist, I was utterly dependent on and totally abandoned to the Spirit. All I could think about was, what if I could not deliver? I had left my job to take this six-month trial position. What if I got fired? How embarrassing it would be.

I know that without God's divine hand in this, we would all be walking away disappointed. But I also knew that it is only out in the deep that the miracles take place. If you stay on the shore, you will never walk on water. It was only when Peter found himself out of his depth that Jesus gave him the invitation to come and do what He did. You see, when we are out in the deep, we can do exactly what Jesus does.

Catching Falling Apples

The birth and growth of Jesus at the Door happened organically and effortlessly. When I first stepped out as a street evangelist, I felt out of my depth and ill-equipped for the task, so I prayed a simple prayer: "Lord, teach me how to fish."

Let me fill in the lines with what that means. It means that everything you will read here has been tested by fire. I did not get it from a book or hear it on a podcast. It comes from firsthand experience.

Although I believe the Lord had placed the office of evangelist upon me from an early age (despite my shunning His advances), it was only when I stepped out onto the streets five days a week for three years that I fully embraced this calling and it fully embraced me. I learned in three years what would normally take people thirty years to learn.

It was a baptism of fire, where I was schooled in evangelism by the Spirit of God, and in that school something beautiful began to happen. The Holy Spirit spoke to me a sentence that was to change the trajectory of my life. He said, *Scott, I want you to imagine these people are all like apples on a tree. When you share, then I'll shake!* Upon hearing that simple phrase, and picturing that simple image, everything changed for me. For the first time in my life I understood what evangelism was—it was an invitation to partnership. It was not about how good or bad I was; it was about how available I was.

This removed the pressure of feeling I had to know everything and convince everyone. It changed me from the inside out as both a disciple and an evangelist.

After my "apple tree" revelation, Jesus' words in John 6:44 (ESV) took on a whole new meaning. There Jesus says, "No one can come to me unless the Father who sent me draws him." The Father, through the power of the Holy Spirit, is drawing people to Him. The Holy Spirit, like a mighty wind, is shaking the trees.

Some apples will move a little, some will not move at all and some (more than you would expect) will fall.

All we have to do is catch. I was not alone in this, and all I had to do was play my part and faithfully share—and the *ruach* wind and breath of heaven would blow accordingly and do the rest. Now when you hear the term "apple tree evangelism," you know what it means.

Everyone is an apple on a tree, as were you until somebody caught you. We are priceless apples waiting to be caught. Whether dirty apples or shiny apples, we are all still apples. Evangelism is as simple as everyday believers going about their business, walking through the apple orchards of life, reaching out their hands to catch the falling apples. Everybody can catch! Yes, even you.

What happens to apples that are ready to fall but nobody catches them? They will either decay and die or fall into the wrong hands. This is the case for every person who is not reached for Jesus by you and me through the power of the Gospel.

It is not dependent on your age, sex or social standing. Young, old, men, women, boys and girls can catch, whether they were born with a silver spoon or a wooden spoon. The thing to remember is that it is not about you anyway; it is about His power on display, which means everybody gets to play.

Now we would have to try extremely hard not to come into contact with any other apples as we go about our daily lives. Just live your life in whatever sphere of influence He has strategically placed you in, and always be willing to catch. You will be privy to apples I will never come into contact with. The orchard of life in which you have been placed has been reserved just for you and entrusted into your care.

Salvation on the Stairwell

Apples are all around us if we will just look up to see them. I was just finishing an Evangelism Made Easy weekend at the mighty

Jake's House Church in Arlington, Washington. After I had spent a long time praying for folks at the altar, I lifted my eyes and right before me was Jose.

The previous evening, I had walked into my hotel, and as I passed by the stairwell to go into my room, I happened to notice a young man. I decided to turn around and go back.

I showed him the picture, but he said, "No English," and motioned for me to walk down the corridor with him.

A little apprehensive, I followed him. He stopped outside his room where two other Mexican, tattoo-bearing, rough-looking lads stood wondering who I was. Neither of them could speak English, so between Google Translate and our Jesus at the Door app, I attempted to walk them through our steps. The other two lads left, but Jose stayed, standing wide-eyed, and when I talked about Jesus knocking on the door of his heart, he was drinking in every word that I was saying.

He looked overwhelmed as the Holy Spirit ushered in his salvation. He read the prayer of salvation in Spanish that was on our app and, afterward, turning to me, he hugged me. I got his phone number and said I would contact him.

The next morning, I sent him a text from my friend's phone inviting him to church on Sunday evening. He wanted to come, so I was able to connect him with a beautiful Spanish couple who offered to go and collect him from his hotel. On the way to church, Jose told them his story. He told them that on Saturday evening after he had met me, he slept like a baby. He said when he had hugged me, he felt pure and clean.

After church we prayed for him, and he was filled with the Holy Spirit and began to speak in tongues. He was so hungry for a Spanish Bible that he had even gone down to the reception desk to ask if they had one. When our friend Maria gave him his own Bible, it was as if he had won the lottery.

For the next month Jose kept in contact with me, and the last I heard he is pressing in to his newfound relationship with Jesus, attending the church where I was speaking that night.

«ACTIV8»

I pray that as you read this, something will shift in your heart and mind, that the Holy Spirit will bring you to a place of utter dependence on Him in the area of evangelism. May any preconceived ideas or thoughts that you do not have what it takes to do this fall off you like scales from your eyes. May you see by His power that it is easy as you share and the Holy Spirit shakes. In Jesus' name, Amen.

TWO

WE SHARE, HE SHAKES

WHEN I FIRST began to evangelize full-time, as I chatted with strangers on the street, the Holy Spirit began impressing me with a picture of Jesus standing at the door of someone's heart. Originally inspired by my grandmother's wall art, I found on the internet a more contemporary version of the classic Holman Hunt painting *The Light of the World*, which is a depiction of Revelation 3:20.

I saved this picture as my screen saver and, as I chatted with strangers on the street, the Holy Spirit dropped into my spirit phrases or points pertaining to it. As I spoke them out, it was like flaming arrows being shot into the hearts of the listeners, and the atmosphere became both charged and changed. I felt so much life in them that I would actually grow impatient for the conversations to end so I could hurriedly record these phrases in my phone.

These God-given keys unlocked something within the stranger and became what we now know as Jesus at the Door—image-laden Gospel-sharing in a matter of minutes from introduction all the way to salvation in a relaxed, nonthreatening manner. In the following months, the Holy Spirit shaped the method that would eventually lead thousands to Jesus one by one, day by day, town by town, nation by nation.

Evangelism itself is the very soil out of which Jesus at the Door grew, contributing factors to its depth of anointing, I am certain. It was birthed in the harvest fields of life—not in a classroom at seminary, around a table of theologians, or even, may I say, in the prayer closet. I did not lock myself away on a 21-day fast seeking God for an evangelistic technique to win the masses; I stepped out in vulnerability and dependency, and Jesus did the rest.

In order to give away what the Spirit gave me, however, we needed our own picture. This artwork comes courtesy of acclaimed artist and author Charlie Mackesy. The image is unbelievably anointed. Still to this day the people I train always come back from their first times out on the streets awestruck by the way others are drawn in by the power of this picture.

Just last month I was in Vienna, Austria, and I stopped a young millennial who immediately told me he was an atheist. Before going his own way, however, he turned to me and asked if he could keep the card.

"Eh, yes, I guess so," I said. I was a little perplexed as to why an apparent atheist would desire a picture of Jesus knocking on the door to his heart. At the same time I was not really surprised, as I had personally witnessed and heard from others about these encounters where individuals were supernaturally fixated on the image, often resulting in their salvation. You know the saying, that a picture paints a thousand words.

Tent L.A. Encounter

In early 2019 the Holy Spirit told me to roll out tent crusades in every major U.S. city, so in August that year our ministry put on Tent L.A. Hiring out Grand Park, we gathered teams of people who had been blessed in some way by Jesus at the Door and were willing to give up their time, money and energy to launch a full-scale ground assault upon the devil and his minions.

We spent three days out on the streets of downtown Los Angeles sharing the Gospel, culminating with three tent gatherings in the evenings. We witnessed 150-plus people accept Christ as we unleashed the unadulterated power of the Gospel upon those city streets.

My team and I engaged a group of people on Friday afternoon in the heart of downtown. The guy I spoke to was called Duke.

"Can I ask you a quick question?" I started, then extended my arm closer to his face so he could see the image. From his seat on the ground, he abruptly plucked the card out of my hand and held it closely before his eyes. He began to mumble as if he was talking to the image, smiling, then laughing. It was clear Duke was having an encounter with the Lord, and I had not even really uttered a word yet.

I tried to walk Duke down the nine steps to salvation, but it was going in one ear and out the other. Quite frankly, he seemed spellbound. I had never experienced anything of this magnitude before. We were there for some time, and I had moved on to his friends, praying for them and leaving Duke to revel in his moment.

Finally, I announced we had to leave, as our tent meeting was beginning shortly. I invited Duke and his friends to join us.

He immediately snapped out of his trance-like state and said, "Yes, I want to come."

He asked us to wait there while he went to get changed, so two of our team waited around to chaperone Duke back to the park, but he never came back. I was a little disappointed.

Fast-forward 24 hours. We were about to begin our Saturday evening meeting, and I recognized a face in the back of the tent. I walked over and introduced myself when it dawned on me: It was Duke. Later, after I shared the Gospel and gave the altar call, Duke, as if he had been waiting for the invitation all evening, shot his hand in the air with fierce gusto.

He came to the front and, turning to look at me with tears in his eyes, he said, "I feel like crying."

He then threw his arms around me tightly. Now, Duke is a six-foot-four African American with a build that resembles a sturdy basketball player, and he was just holding me.

You could have heard a pin drop in that tent. Those in attendance were on the edge of their seats as this haunting silence filled the atmosphere. It felt as if the whole of heaven and the great cloud of witnesses were paused, holding their breath, looking on in anticipation right before their salvation celebrations were to begin (see Luke 15:7). It must have been sixty seconds of silence before this big dude we met in the 'hood of downtown L.A. let me go.

There were others at the altar praying also, and I announced, "Who wants to be baptized?"

Duke looked at me and said, "Yes, I do!"

Well, to be honest, the language he used was more American-street and less Queen's English. It was more like, "You know, that's what's up."

Other brand-new believers from the past couple of days echoed Duke's response and, like a little mob of misfits, upon hearing my command, "Everyone to the fountain," we all urgently made our way to the fountain at the top of the park. We baptized Duke, along with some of the others who had accepted Christ that weekend, all because of a picture.

Clearly, it is no ordinary picture.

The Power of a Picture

One Friday afternoon I arrived at the airport, excited for where I was going. The plan was for me to partner with Brian "Head" Welch, lead guitarist of the metal band Korn, in presenting the Gospel after one of their concerts, but God had plans for me before I even got there.

I stood in the line of passengers waiting to pass through the checkpoint into the security line, which required scanning your boarding pass. Mine was on my phone, and as I turned my phone upside down to match the barcodes on my app with the scanning machine, a security guard happened to glance over to see my phone case, which has a large image of Jesus knocking upon a heart's door (the same that we have on our card).

He made his way over, loudly exclaiming, "Hey, what's that on your phone cover?"

I was running a little late but discerned it was a Holy Spirit–inspired moment, so I told him exactly what it was and began to walk him down the nine steps to salvation. Midway through, an alarm started going off.

When I asked what it was as it was very off-putting, he just said, "It's okay, carry on. That's just because I'm leaning over here talking to you."

Other travelers were also scanning their own boarding passes and, at times, asking for his assistance. He ignored them completely.

He felt the Holy Spirit as I prayed for him and accepted Christ right there and then. All this was happening at the entrance to the barriers that I was yet to pass. I remember being conscious that even in this potentially awkward and haphazard moment, the Spirit of God was present, longing to make His appeal for reconciliation through me as Christ's ambassador (see 2 Corinthians 5:19–20).

Our security guard certainly got caught up in what was his very own Kingdom encounter. I have heard it said that the awesome is in the awkward, and it was certainly true in that moment.

Simple Points to Remember

These stories illustrate just how much this strategy relies on God and not on us. If this were about us being clever, we could never design a picture that, all by itself, leads unbelievers to encounter

Jesus in life-changing ways. No picture does that alone without the power of God working through it, and, truly, no evangelist leads anyone to Jesus without the power of God working through him or her either.

Moving then from the picture to the card, let me clarify that our Jesus at the Door Equipping Card is not a tract—you do not give it away. It is fashioned solely so the believer can engage another individual in conversation and walk that person down the nine steps to salvation.

Also, it is important not to resist the order of the prompts. You will find that it is designed in this succinct way to make things smooth for you.

Remember, it is not a monologue; it is a dialogue. Christianity is relational. We do not want them just to stand there while we verbally open fire on them.

The Approach

Now, let's dive a bit deeper into the first prompt you will use to engage someone in conversation about the picture.

For starters, before you can use the prompt, you need to approach someone with the intent of starting a conversation that will quickly lead to salvation.

Many people ask me, "How do you know which people to ask? Does the Holy Spirit point out the ripe ones?"

In short, no. Well, not at the beginning, anyway.

Remember everyone is an apple. Approach anyone and everyone in a quest to find the ripe ones. This does not mean to run around like a headless chicken here, there and everywhere; it means notice the people who come across your path day to day. The more you work with your partner, the Holy Spirit, the more you become tuned in to where He is moving, and you can follow accordingly.

As you walk up to an individual, be polite and ask permission to start a conversation. Something like, "Excuse me, can I ask you a quick question?" works best. The way people respond will also reveal how ready they are.

If they say no at any point, honor their no. Do not keep pushing in order to accomplish a job. Jesus did only what He saw the Father doing (see John 5:19), and we do only what we see the Spirit doing, so approach it with an open hand. Do not hold on too tight or put pressure on yourself.

Sometimes it is just not your apple. When an apple is not ready to fall, move on to find an apple that is ready. We share, God shakes, and the ripe apples will fall.

To illustrate that, I can tell you that during my time on staff as a street evangelist we were daily seeing heaven invade earth—it was revival town. One morning, however, I approached twenty people, one after the other, each one turning me away before I could begin.

At first it knocked my confidence, so I paused momentarily to reflect. Then, right in that place, I stopped to thank the Lord. I thanked Him for showing me twenty apples that were not ready to fall and for saving my time, energy and focus for the ones that were about to fall. Then, sure enough, very soon after that, one by one they began to fall.

Sometimes It Is Not Your Apple

Now, in case you find yourself in a similar situation, here is the danger: You walk away from those twenty unripe apples feeling rejection, feeling as if you do not have the "gift," so you retreat, defeated, questioning whether this is what you are called to do. This is a common way for the devil to take people out.

People will often ask me, "How do you handle rejection?"

I always reply, "Are they your apples?"

The answer is, no, they are not; you do not own them, so why are you taking it so personally? Let the Lord of the harvest (see Matthew 9:38) worry about His apples. You just work hard at what He has asked you to do faithfully. Take your eyes off of you, the laborer (see 1 Corinthians 3:9), and put them on the Father, who is the Gardener (see John 15:1). You just catch the apples as they fall from the trees He has already pruned.

Jesus did only what He saw the Father doing (see John 5:19), and we do only what we see the Spirit doing.

Again, approach it with an open hand and do not hold on too tight or put pressure on yourself.

If I could sum up *evangelism* in one sentence, it would be: Giving up *all* control so that He can take *full* control.

Sometimes it is just not your apple. When the apple is not ready to fall, you may well feel inclined to want to swing metaphorically on the branch in a bid to make it fall, instead of moving on to find an apple that is ready to fall. Do not fall into this trap. We are not looking to pin somebody to the floor by winning a verbal wrestling match on the subjects of science, spaceships, monkeys or matter.

It will bleed you dry of your energy and, more importantly, will stop you from catching those ripe apples that are ready to be caught.

If you can talk people into being Christians, someone else can talk them out of it. It is not down to your rhetorical prowess; what they need is a power encounter. That can only happen when you introduce them to the One with all the power—your Partner.

The Opening Words

If people say yes when you approach them, ask, "Have you seen this picture before, and do you pray?"

Lay down the foundation for the whole conversation—the picture. This is the centerpiece for all you will share, so hold it aloft for them to see throughout your conversation. It also helps because if people feel nervous, they often like to stare at it instead of you.

If they say no to the question, "Do you ever pray?," then notice the words on the card in parentheses to help you dig deeper. You can ask, "Do you pray in emergencies or during difficult times in life?" If the answer is yes, then move on to the next prompt.

If the answer is no, then ask, "Do you believe God is there?" If the answer is yes, then move to the next prompt. But if the answer is no once again—unless you hear something from the Spirit—say, "Well, He believes in you," bless them and continue your search.

Never assume just because someone does not pray that he or she will not be interested in God. I have led lots of people to Jesus who never prayed, but still believed in God.

And on the other hand, never assume just because someone prays that he or she is a Christian. One young lady I trained walked up to a young mother and asked her, "Have you seen this picture before, and do you pray?"

The young mother replied, "Yes, I pray," to which my trainee replied, "Oh, so you are a Christian?"

The young mom said yes, so my trainee thanked her and ended the conversation, and the mom began to walk away.

But I called out to her, "Excuse me!"

She came back, and I continued where my trainee had left off, walking her through the nine steps. We discovered that she was not a Christian at all—though she identified more with that label than as a Muslim or a Buddhist—but she did pray every evening before going to bed. We could have assumed she was already a Christian, but instead we were able to lead her to Christ.

Trust the process and, whenever possible, complete the process. Never assume you know where someone is spiritually, but start at the beginning and keep leading until you lead that person to Jesus.

Easter Egg Hunt

My kids love Easter egg hunts. My wife and I hide the eggs all around the house and the kids try excitedly to find them. They always find the easily positioned ones first (the low-hanging fruit); then as it gets a little harder, their momentum slows. No matter how long it takes them, however, they never come to my wife or me saying, "I do not want to do this any longer. I give up." No, they know their eggs are there somewhere, so they keep persisting until they find them.

«ACTIV8»

I pray that you, too, will become an apple tree evangelist faithfully extending your arms out to catch those falling apples in whatever sphere of influence the Father, in His infinite wisdom, has placed you. In Jesus' name, Amen.

THREE

YOUR NAVIGATION
TO SALVATION

THINK OF THE last time you got into your car. Did you know where you were going and how you were going to get there? If not, then you probably used a GPS, right?

A Global Positioning System is designed to help you travel by the quickest, easiest route. By following the step-by-step instructions of your navigator, you arrive at your destination. It requires focus and concentration, however, as any other voice except that of your navigator will cause distraction. You will not be singing along to your favorite worship song or listening to your favorite preacher. In this moment you have capacity for only one voice.

Once you arrive at your destination, though, the thought of repeating the journey is not so daunting. The next time you are more relaxed, knowing you have been there before. With the directions stored in your memory bank, you can crank up the worship music, lose yourself in your favorite teaching and enjoy the ride.

Similarly, Jesus at the Door will act as your very own evangelistic GPS, your navigation to salvation, showing you where you need to go and exactly how to get there, simply by following the nine-point directions. Then once you memorize the nine power points, it will free you up—not to listen to your favorite worship song or preacher, but to listen to the voice of your evangelism partner, the Holy Spirit. My aim is to bring you to a place where you can easily walk a person to the destination of salvation without even breaking a sweat, where it becomes so second nature that no matter what is going on around you, you are able to maintain your composure and focus at all times.

You see, in this moment all your senses are stimulated and firing on all cylinders. There are so many moving pieces, variables, distractions baying for your attention—cars whizzing by, people walking around you, noises, smells and sounds—that you could potentially be knocked off balance. All these things and more happen while we drive to work every day, yet think about it. Have you ever mentally slipped into autopilot and, before you know it, you are there already?

Despite the distractions, you get to a place of being so mentally relaxed that you drive without effort. We can reach the same place in evangelism where we are so relaxed that it just spills out of us. I believe that whatever fills you, spills out of you.

Salvation at Thirty Thousand Feet

I was on a flight, and not long into the flight the lady in front of me got up from her seat.

The Holy Spirit spoke to my heart: *This lady is ready for Me.*

Shortly after, she leaned over the back of her seat, looked me straight in the eyes (ignoring the other two passengers sitting beside me) and uttered for all to hear, "I am in so much pain!"

Wow, okay, that is a pretty clear open door my partner, the Holy Spirit, is presenting me, I thought.

I offered to pray for her. She explained how she is ex-military and how she was blown up in a car explosion while on patrol. It was now five back operations later, and she had been officially classified as an invalid.

I moved to where she was, knelt down beside her and told her, "Before I pray for you, I want to show you something." I proceeded to walk her through Jesus at the Door. I did this because I believe the sickness in her body was secondary to the sickness in her soul. She felt the presence of Jesus at thirty thousand feet and prayed to accept Christ, telling me she had been wanting to find God.

I then prayed for her back to be healed, commanding all pain to leave in Jesus' name. She said immediately that she felt heat filling her back and the pain leaving.

When the plane landed, I asked her, "How does your back feel?"

She replied in disbelief and glee, "I have no pain!" and gave me her phone number so I could help her get connected to a local church. When I arrived at my hotel I messaged her and she replied immediately, telling me how her neighbor came around to see her and was amazed to find her mobile and without pain.

From Rolling a Joint to Tears of Repentance

Another time, I had been invited to a Vineyard Records songwriters' retreat in Herefordshire, England. As our train neared the platform at Hereford, I noticed two lads smoking weed, adorned in thick gold chains with a big bulldog by their side. They looked like what we refer to in the U.K. as *scallys* (meaning scallywags).

Leaving the train, I felt the Lord directing me to talk to them, so I went onto the street. I noticed one of the lads was sitting alone rolling a joint. I asked him for a taxi number and began to talk with him. I could not help noticing a gash across the right side of his face and asked him what happened. He told me he had been glassed in the face in a fight two days earlier. He was in constant pain and could not sleep. I told him Jesus could take the pain away and asked if I could pray for him. He agreed, so I asked him to stand and put his spliff away out of respect while we prayed, which he did.

All this was happening as we stood outside a busy train station. I love these organic Kingdom appointments.

I prayed and God answered. It was a holy moment as this young man stood with his eyes closed and the Spirit of God touched his life. He began rocking back and forth as the peace of Christ washed over him, and he said, "For the first time in two days I feel I could sleep right here and now." I continued to pray that the Lord would touch his heart and he started crying. I then shared the Gospel, which he had never heard, and he opened the door of his heart to Jesus.

At the exact moment we finished praying, my taxi pulled up, just in time for the young man to give me his number.

The Gospel Is the Vehicle to Drive You There

There are a number of layers hidden in this second story. Let's see how they worked together to help this young man open the door of his heart to Jesus.

First, I felt the Holy Spirit prompting me to approach him. This instance was before I had the nine steps of Jesus at the Door, so I engaged him by asking a question I needed to ask someone anyway. It was a natural interaction. Think of all the people you see each week who fit that description.

Then I just carried on the conversation. He had a gash on his face, so it was natural to show interest and concern. His injury was also an easy opportunity to ask him if I could pray for him. As you begin to look, you will be amazed how often this sort of opportunity presents itself to you.

The next thing I knew, God was moving, so I explained that Jesus was knocking at the door of his heart. When he realized that the choice was his alone, he wanted to let Jesus in. So this ripe apple fell right into salvation.

In the GPS metaphor, the Gospel is always the vehicle and salvation is always the destination. So often nowadays people seem to celebrate healings or the prophetic as though supernatural ministry were the goal. I tell you, leading someone to open the door of his heart is supernatural ministry!

Prophecy and healings are wonderful. I was eager to pray for God to heal this young man. They can be like extra gears in the car to help you arrive more quickly to the destination, yet without the car (the Gospel), they will not take you to your destination (salvation). The truth is, even the best prophetic word or most miraculous healing will not change someone's life in the light of eternity.

Marry these supernatural tools to the Gospel to add a dimension of power to your proclamation, but let the Gospel drive you to your destination.

The Garden Where All Other Gifts Grow

God drove this point home to me one night when I heard the Holy Spirit say: *Jesus at the Door is a garden where all your other gifts can grow.* You see I am not saying anyone should abandon the prophetic or healing, but allow them to grow in the soil of salvation.

We have to remember, the point of the prophetic, healing and evangelistic ministries is to lead an individual into relationship with God. As with any relationship, we become like those we spend time with, and the more time we spend with them, the more we will get to know them.

The Holy Spirit is the best prophet, healer and evangelist, so the more time you spend with Him, the more you will become like

Him. You cannot have an evangelism partner like the Holy Spirit and not get better at words of knowledge, healing and evangelism.

This is exactly how it happened with me. I stood on a street five days a week, spending time with my evangelism partner, the Holy Spirit. After some months I found I began to know more of how He thinks, feels and moves.

You see, you can know the Holy Spirit in your prayer closet, quiet time or Bible study, but it is a totally different thing to know Him in the harvest fields. Knowing His voice in the fields of life will only come through time together and experience, and this will only happen when you place yourself in a situation where you become totally dependent on Him to meet you there.

In Jesus at the Door we encourage and promote both the prophetic and healing. What some may find a little different, however, is that we do not make them the driving force.

If you do not yet move fluidly in the prophetic or healing, simply by engaging with Jesus at the Door you are automatically aligning yourself with the Giver of those gifts. Either way, the Gospel is enough.

Jesus at the Door Changed My Life

I have a dear friend named Chris Donald, who is one of four pastors at the Promise Church in Woodland, Washington. This is, incidentally, the church my family and I are part of now.

For the past couple of years, Chris has been working for Todd White, serving as the lead pastor and evangelist, helping to run his school, Lifestyle Christianity University (LCU), in Dallas.

When Chris got tuned in to Jesus at the Door, he was instantly won over by it. He began to use it, merging it with what he had been doing the past thirteen years as an evangelist in his own right, which was prophetic healing. This was a big change for him, because he had become accomplished in prophetic healing. It was hard, at first, for Chris really to flow in this new method of ours. In many ways he had to start again, go low and trust that what the Lord had given me in Jesus at the Door was indeed straight from Him.

Then in 2018, Chris and I went to India together, launching Jesus at the Door over there. I sat on a two-hour bus ride with Chris. He was determined to learn the nine points verbatim by the time he got off the bus, and that is exactly what he did.

Chris went on to take Jesus at the Door to churches in the U.S., empowering believers in this reaping-style evangelism. He became our biggest advocate, proudly telling anyone who asks, "Jesus at the Door changed my life." Like me, Chris credits Jesus at the Door with turning him from a sowing evangelist into a reaping evangelist.

Chris did not stop there. He also captured our heart's desire for follow-up and making disciples. He now not only leads people daily to the destination point of salvation, but after adopting our framework for our New Believers group, he began one out of LCU, which is something they previously had not done. It is growing from strength to strength. In the past eight months alone, they have baptized more than 170 people and are seeing lives transformed as they get plugged into their church community.

From Humility to Breakthrough

Whether you are stepping out for the first time to do the work of an evangelist or you are a seasoned pro, following these simple steps will make you more fruitful.

It will, however, require a level of humility on your part. There are well-known evangelists who travel the world and have embraced Jesus at the Door, training people in it as they go, but not everyone was as quick as Chris to adopt our method.

In order for Chris to get his breakthrough, he had to humble himself, which is hard. Chris had a way that he knew could get

him to a certain place, yet he was the first to admit that his way
was not as effective in getting him to that desired destination point
of salvation.

Whether you are moving in prophetic healing like Chris, or
maybe some other approach, I firmly believe what the Lord has
given in these steps to salvation will make anyone more fruitful.
Just try it.

——《ACTIV8》——

Lord, I pray that daily we will see the opportunities You are presenting and follow the "navigation to salvation" directions You provide
to help hearts open to you. In Jesus' name, Amen.

FOUR

WHY RELATIONSHIP?

THIS IS THE third prompt on the Jesus at the Door Equipping Card. If you find yourself at this point, it means the individual has responded yes to either of the opening questions—Do you pray? or Do you believe God is there? It also means the person understands that the handle of the door to let Jesus in is on the inside.

My question for you is, How many people do you know who pray before they go to sleep? How many people do you know who believe there is a God? Through this third prompt, we are trying to make a clear distinction between religion and relationship. You see, religion happens outside the door and relationship happens inside.

When I first began this teaching, some people advised me to change point three to make it softer and more palatable. They felt that telling somebody "You do not know God personally" was too direct, but they were missing the point. The Gospel is confrontational; it demands a response. When presented properly, it should rouse a response one way or the other.

It stirs up a kind of offended response from the believer, who would object, "I do know Him personally!" This is by design. There are a couple of significant junctures when the born-again believer can "out" him or herself, and this is one of them.

Talking Through the Door

For that person, however, who knows God is there—somewhere—who maybe prays every night before going to sleep, or even attends church on occasion, yet does not have a personal relationship with Jesus, the Holy Spirit will stir something on the inside in response to the provocative nature of this statement, rousing some kind of response.

You will also find yourself in situations where you meet religious people who will tell you they pray and believe in God. Many of these will present their code of ethics, practices and overall religiosity as the reason for their right standing with God. Let's say, however, that you discern they do not have a relationship with Jesus. What do you do?

You need to confront them with the truth and challenge them head-on, all of which you can do without discrediting them.

Eternity in Your Heart

What I am about to share is what I would call the most valuable step that is outside of our nine points. It is an excellent gut check for anyone who believes in God but does not know Him, even for those trusting religious practices.

We ask the individual, "If you died tonight (which I pray you do not), could you say with a hundred percent certainty, beyond a shadow of a doubt, that you would go to heaven?" Now, 99.9 percent of people who have not yet been sealed with the stamp of salvation will respond with, "Nobody could say that for sure."

You see, they have yet to receive eternity into their hearts (see Ecclesiastes 3:11). They have not yet been covered by His atoning blood. Some will tell you, "Yes, I know for sure," even though you can tell they do not. That is just their way of letting you know they do not want to proceed any further.

When people are challenged in their core beliefs, they will either embrace it or resist it. Like a fire, people will be drawn to its warmth or run from it to avoid being burnt. If they admit they do not have that assurance, I then tell them, "Let's say I gave you my phone as a gift and you took it home with you. A family member might ask you, 'Is that your phone?' You would reply, 'Yes, this person came up to me and gave it to me,' right? Well, the Bible says that the gift of God is eternal life [see Romans 6:23], and when you get it, you know you have it. I can tell you with a hundred percent certainty I know I am going to heaven when I die. What you are doing is talking to God through the door."

The innate design in the heart of man is to be in union with God, but the devil has twisted this to trick people into feeling they have to work at it. So many Scriptures speak to this, including these, just to list a few:

> We are all infected and impure with sin. When we display our righteous deeds, they are nothing but filthy rags.
>
> Isaiah 64:6

> "These people honor me with their lips, but their hearts are far from me."
>
> Matthew 15:8

> They will act religious, but they will reject the power that could make them godly.
>
> 2 Timothy 3:5

Our Evangelism Partner

A while back, I had been in Europe equipping churches in evangelism. I sat at the airport waiting to board a flight home, hoodie up and earphones on. I had mentally switched off and was looking forward to a long sleep on the plane. When it was time to board, I made my way to the line of passengers and felt the nudge of the Spirit prodding me to talk to the mother and daughter who stood behind me.

Honestly, I did not want to talk to anyone, so I reasoned with myself that maybe it was not the Lord after all. Like a shepherd herding sheep, the airline staff began to direct us forward to a waiting tunnel; there seemed to be some kind of holdup. It was only fifteen minutes, but those fifteen minutes felt like hours as my flesh wrestled every minute with my spirit as the Lord kept prodding me to talk with them.

During my inner turmoil, the mother tapped me on the shoulder.

"I like your jacket," she said, smiling.

It was a Jesus at the Door jacket. What a perfect segue into walking her down the steps to salvation—but no, I smiled and replied, "Thank you," before turning back around. Even writing this, I am shocked I acted this way; it is so not like me, but the Lord was about to teach me a valuable lesson.

Eventually, after letting those behind me pass by while I got some things from my case, I made my way onto the plane. Looking for my seat number I could see in the distance the same mother and daughter already sitting. I thought, *I wonder . . . nah, it could not be*, but as I moved past every aisle to my designated seat, the odds that we were about to sit together became intrinsically higher. Sure enough, in a grouping of three seats, there was my seat waiting for me right next to theirs.

Okay, Lord, I get it now. I am sorry.

I sat down, introduced myself and began to share the life-changing Gospel message. For the next three hours of the flight, we were enveloped in our Father's embrace.

Carol, the mother, had left Northern Ireland as a young lady (now in her late fifties) after falling in love and marrying an American businessman. She had been exposed to religion but never really had much time for God. She had begun to go to church of late and was softening to God, but it was all still distant for her.

That is why when I began to walk her through the picture and nine points, her face lit up. You see, Jesus at the Door was birthed on the streets of Northern Ireland. It was born into a religious culture where people know a lot about God (religion), but they do not know Him personally (relationship).

Carol and her family had been blessed with a good life, but something terrible had happened recently that had sent them into a tailspin, leaving them feeling all alone, longing for comfort and in need of counsel. It just so happened that she was about to encounter both the Comforter and Counselor.

Their son, Andrew, had very recently taken his own life, which is why Carol was back in her motherland for the first time in many years. She was going to see her family. I prayed for them, they cried, we hugged, I prayed some more, and Jesus made Himself known.

Carol was not quite ready to accept Jesus in that moment, but she had been so impacted by our time together that she asked if she could keep the Jesus at the Door card. Of course, I obliged.

I left feeling very sorry before the Lord for nearly missing that opportunity, and yet thankful at the same time for the Lord's mighty hand of providence in all of it. It was another reminder that the Holy Spirit is our evangelism partner. He is weaving together a beautiful tapestry and we are like the needle in His hand. He gently holds us, weaving us in and out of encounters in a fluid motion. We do not know what the finished piece of art will look like, but I love to be that needle in His holy hands, surrendered to go this way and that as He directs.

Carving His Name on Hearts

Carol's story was not done. Six months after that flight, I received this email on our website:

> Hi, Scott. I believe it was you my daughter and I sat beside in late June on a flight. My son, Andrew, had died suddenly. Our hearts have been shattered and our very close family unit forever traumatized by the loss of sweet and sensitive Andrew. We are still in shock and disbelief, although trying to keep hope and trust in God as we walk through each day seeking Him for strength, courage and acceptance. We had spent four weeks traveling and visiting family and friends, and the entire time not one person prayed with us or acknowledged our loss to the extent that it provided any one of us comfort. It was heartbreaking and disappointing.
>
> Until we met you. We shared our story and you inspired us with your testimony, your love of Jesus and the Gospel and witness to the transformative impact it has had on so many lives. You prayed with us, and from that encounter we have been encouraged to just trust and to seek an intimate relationship with Jesus and our heavenly Father. On my son Andrew's headstone, we had a picture of Jesus at the Door engraved. I have opened the door to Jesus.
>
> I thank you from the bottom of my heart.
>
> I thank God for the lives you have reached and hearts you have opened. God bless you and your ministry. With my deepest gratitude, Carol.

It was Charles Spurgeon who said, "Carve your name on hearts, not on marble." Little did I know that after carving the name of Jesus upon this family's heart that it would lead to His name also being carved on marble.

«ACTIV8»

Lord, I thank You that every day all around our world people are crying out to meet You. Many just do not know it is You they are looking for until we make the introduction. Give Your child reading this the tenacity to press into the places You are pointing out, surrendered to You and Your Gospel. In Jesus' name, Amen.

FIVE

PEDALING THE GOSPEL

IF YOU LOOK at the Jesus at the Door Equipping Card, you will see that we are stepping into the Red Zone, which is aptly colored, to address sin. If those we are trying to reach will not acknowledge their sin, why would they acknowledge their need of a Savior?

If you are going to get any pushback while leading someone through the card, it is going to be here. This is because the Bible tells us that the Gospel is foolishness to those that are perishing (see 1 Corinthians 1:18) and that our godly lives are "a dreadful smell of death and doom" to those same people (2 Corinthians 2:16).

When it comes to evangelism, many within the Church view sin as the proverbial hot potato that they do not like to touch. You see, when we broach the subject of sin, we are going beyond the veil, so to speak; we are challenging those we approach to look at how far they have fallen short of God's standard in their lives. This does not happen when we simply pray for the sick, share our testimonies or tell people how much Jesus loves them. You cannot truly share the Gospel without facing sin head-on.

Sin Is Universal . . . and So Is the Holy Spirit

As I have traveled to various nations sharing the Gospel and equipping the Body of Christ in evangelism, I have found two things to be true: Sin is universal, and so is the Holy Ghost.

I was in Australia earlier this year and had only been there minutes when I engaged someone in conversation to share the Gospel. I had a revelation: Australia has sinners also. As the Spirit of God fell on the man I was witnessing to, I immediately had a second revelation: The Holy Spirit had beat me to Australia.

I am sure you are familiar with the saying, "I hope God shows up." This is a Christianese term many use to express their desire for the Lord to make Himself manifestly present, be it in worship, Sunday services or wherever.

When it comes to evangelism, you never need to say, "I hope God shows up." He is already there hoping you show up.

A month later I was in South Africa. Again within a short time of being there I shared the Gospel with someone, and it happened again, another light bulb moment: South Africa also has sinners, and—yes, you guessed it—the Holy Spirit had also beat me to South Africa.

What does this mean? It means that whenever these two get within close proximity of each other, fireworks go off. You see, the Holy Spirit is the perfect antidote to sin. Every encounter is a potential fireworks show for which you have been given a front row seat.

There Is Nothing in My Backpack

Let's imagine you engage an individual in conversation and, in answer to this first question about the weight of sin in his backpack, he replies, "There would be nothing in my bag." Now, we know he is lying, and he knows he is lying. The Bible states clearly that "*all* have sinned and fall short" (Romans 3:23 ESV, emphasis added). This is just a person's way of letting you know he or she does not wish to proceed any further.

We know that everyone is included in the "all," so why will some people not admit it? Maybe we should sit them down for five minutes and dredge up all their sins from the past week and make them feel really bad. Then would they see it?

There are some evangelism techniques that adopt this kind of method. This is meant as no slight against them because everything has its place, but John 16:8 tells us that the Holy Spirit will convict the world of sin. I ask you: If they will not listen to Him, why on earth would we assume they will listen to us? Everything we do is through the lens of our Captain.

That said, it is important in order to avoid any ambiguity here that we are very clear exactly what it is we are trying to say through our question. We are not saying it is either a heavy bag or nothing at all.

Some people, for example, reply, "No, my bag wouldn't be heavy." I have seen some who are evangelizing terminate the conversation here, thinking, *Okay, this person is not my apple.*

What you want to say next instead is: "Would there be anything in your backpack?"

I often reassure those I talk to by telling them everyone would have something in his bag—nobody is perfect. It is funny how many people beat me to it and respond with the exact same comment.

You may wonder why we have to be so direct about sin. Might we offend them? We might, but it is imperative that they take ownership of their sin if they are to take ownership of their need for a Savior.

She Felt Clean

During a trip to England, I was equipping a group of people with these tools and we all ventured out onto the streets to put them into practice. I approached a young mom pushing her stroller and tried to engage her in conversation.

She looked at me and said, "I do not speak English." She then said "Portuguese?"

One of the men standing next to me interjected, "I speak Portuguese. I am from Brazil." With his head bowed, he began to read the card for her. As he landed on the Red Zone, he asked her, "Visualize wearing a backpack. If we filled it with all your sin, would it be heavy?" He looked up.

"Yes," she said.

He bent his head back down and continued to read. She started weeping, but because he was doing exactly what I had taught him, which was to read the card, he did not notice what was unfolding before his eyes—this beautiful Kingdom moment where the gentle conviction of the Holy Ghost showed this wandering, shepherd-less soul the weight of her sin, followed by a taste of the love of God. He continued to the end, and she prayed with him to make Jesus the Lord of her life.

Speaking through my now-bewildered brother, I asked her, "What was it that made you cry?"

She said she felt a weight lifting off her shoulders. At the end I asked her how she felt, and she replied with one word: Clean!

Never Tell Them What They Believe

Jesus at the Door presents a gentle approach that packs one heck of a punch. One afternoon on the campus of Portland (Oregon) State University, in what is known as one of America's least-churched regions, a student said, "I've had people speak to me about God before, but this approach has been my favorite. I didn't feel you were shoving it down my throat."

This was especially interesting, as we face sin head-on probably more than most when sharing.

It is helpful to know that at no point during the nine-step process do we presume to tell the listeners what they believe. We simply share in partnership with the Shaker, presenting the options to them and waiting for them to tell us which ones, if any, pertain to them. For example:

1. *Do you pray/believe?* We are not presuming or telling them that they do.
2. *Would your bag be heavy with your sin?* We are not saying their bag is heavy.
3. *If Jesus were here, would you let Him in?* We are asking if they have faith to believe He is here. We are only going as far as their level of faith allows us.

Everything we do follows a pathway: First, acknowledgment/ belief in God; second, awareness and admittance of his or her own sin; third, acceptance of Jesus in order to bring it to completion.

We Share, He Shakes—We Ride, He Waits

If we share and He shakes, then we ride and He waits.

Tandem bicycles are built for two people (bear with me; it gets better). The person at the front is called the captain, and the captain has two jobs. The first job is to hold the bicycle upright so the person at the back can climb on, and the second is to navigate the course. The rear rider is called the stoker, derived from the phrase "to stoke a fire." That person has one job—to pedal.

The Holy Spirit spoke to me through this analogy, showing me that He is the Captain and that every day He waits for us (stokers) to begin pedaling (stoking the fire), so that He can take us on our daily adventure. He will direct our every move, as Isaiah 45:2 says: "I will go before you." We just have to move.

This means that when we get out of bed each day, the Holy Spirit is there on that bicycle, and He is saying, "Jump on! Let's go and change the world together."

Sometimes we are praying, "Lord, please move in my father, mother, brother, sister or best friend's life. Please do something in my community." We are crying out for a move of God, and He is crying out for a move from you.

Removing the Pressure of Performance

Tandem bicycles are a perfect illustration of biblical New Testament partnership. The captain, desiring the stoker's partnership, handicaps himself by depending on the stoker to move. Then, likewise, the stoker shows the same dependency as he pedals blindly, his only sight being the back of his captain, whose eyes he trusts to lead him in the right direction.

Every move I make, every single person I approach, I do it through the lens of my Captain. I stop an individual to ask a question, which means I stop pedaling momentarily. The person's response reveals to me whether or not my Captain wants to linger there. If not, I simply begin to pedal again. I take a refusal to mean this is simply someone who is not being drawn today. Otherwise, we all would have stopped. This removes the pressure of performance.

On Your Bike!

A few years ago, I met a man who was new to our church, and he had big dreams. He said, "The Lord's going to provide a bus for me. Once He does, I am going to go to some of the roughest housing projects and share the Gospel."

I thought for a moment, then replied, "Okay, great, but while you are waiting for your bus, why don't you go on your bike? If you don't have a bike, go on foot."

Sadly, he was offended by my comments. Many years passed, and he was still without a bus—because he never moved.

Do not be so focused on your grand, future dreams that you forget to take small steps today. Just put one foot in front of the other and move.

That is how we all ride bicycles—by moving one leg, immediately followed by the other. It is just like walking.

What is interesting is that if you start out riding in a high gear, it is difficult to pedal. But as soon as you begin to move, you gather momentum quickly. Soon you find that you are not even focusing on riding a bike. You are just enjoying the journey.

It is the same with evangelism. For some the initial cost will be greater, but does that not make the sacrifice unto our Lord that much sweeter?

The Great Co-Mission

In 1 Corinthians 3:9, the apostle Paul describes us as co-laborers in the proclamation of the Gospel. Scripture is full of this wonderful imagery where the Lord gives of Himself, and at times even handicaps Himself, in order for those He loves to participate in His plans and purposes on the earth.

I cannot think of any example more comparable than that of the Great Commission—the most monumental of mandates entrusted into the hands of a melting pot of rough, ragtag fishermen, tax collectors and women of ill repute. Jesus entrusted the mass globalization of the Gospel to a mob of misfits. But He did not leave them to do it alone. Jesus gave His Church the promised Holy Spirit so we could partner with Him (see Acts 2).

This gift of the Holy Spirit imparted a new boldness and desire to obey Him. The Great Commission, found in Matthew 28:18–20, is where Jesus instructs His disciples to "go and make disciples of all nations." This is not called the Great Mission, because it is an invitation to partnership. This *co*-mission could have been called the Great Invitation, an all-inclusive Gospel adventure of extreme proportions extended to every man, woman and child who bears His name. Presented with the opportunity to partner with Him and play a part in the redemption of mankind, who can refuse?

Partnership Is Power

In Luke 5, we read the story of the first disciples where Jesus told Peter to go out where it is deeper and let down his nets. Peter retorts, "We worked hard all last night and did not catch a thing. But if you say so, I will let the nets down again" (verse 5). The catch was so great that Peter's nets began to tear.

What was the reason Peter was able to fill his nets to overflowing? What was the secret of Peter's success? I believe the answer is partnership. You see, the first time Peter had fished alone, but the next time he fished in partnership with Jesus. Power is birthed out of partnership. Partnership is power, and catching requires partnership.

You bring the partnership, and He will bring the power. Peter went in partnership with the Word that had become flesh. The rest is history.

Proclamation Over Personality

Jesus said, "Come follow Me; I will lead the way. I will be your Captain. All you have to do is move your legs. Stay so close that all you can see is My back and we will be good."

As I write this, I hear someone thinking: *Hold up; I am not an evangelist like you. I am an introvert. I am not good around people.*

Let me answer your question with a question: When the fire of the Holy Spirit fell in the Upper Room on the day of Pentecost, do you think it is safe to say that some of the 120 were not gung-ho, type-A personalities, screaming, "Let's change the world for

Jesus!"? I am sure there were some introverts, people of a more timid persuasion who were more comfortable in the background.

What is really interesting is that the Spirit was not in any way dissuaded by their character disposition. He did not seem to think that was a deal breaker. The flame did not fall on Peter, Andrew and Philip, and then the Lord was, like, "Oh, skip that one. Okay, continue with James, Thomas and Nathanael. Oh, now skip this one." No, when the flame fell, it was no respecter of persons. Everyone got set ablaze. Why? Because everyone has been called.

The Great Commission was not given to evangelists; it was given to disciples. This explains why Jesus gave it as a command and not a suggestion. He was not setting the bar so unattainably high that only a few select superstar Christians could attain it. If you are a disciple of Jesus Christ reading this, then you are called to go and make disciples.

Jesus is not cruel. He would never call you to a task without first equipping you with what you need to get the job done. This means He knows something you do not. He knows that He can put a flame upon you so bright and so burning hot that it can empower even the most introverted, intimidated and inactive to light up the whole world. He did not seem to think that your character disposition was reason for an intermission in your involvement with the Great Commission.

Apply Your B-O And G-O

When you were born again, the Bible says you became a brand-new creation (see 2 Corinthians 5:17). In that moment you were endowed with a new Kingdom DNA, whether or not your character disposition or personality type aligns itself to this calling.

Part of that new makeup included B-O. Every single Christian on the planet has it (granted, some more than others). I am talking about Boldness and Obedience. So, if you are reading this, saying, "You do not know how shy I am," or, "You do not know about my anxiety around strangers," then my reply is, "Apply your B-O and G-O!"

Charles, in his sixties, attended my training in England. He was inspired by what he heard and going out with the team during our breakout sessions. He asked his wife if she would give him some moral support, and they went door knocking together in their suburban neighborhood. As a result, Charles got to lead his first person to Jesus in 48 years. Now there is no stopping him.

Imagine that your left leg is Boldness and your right leg is Obedience. Begin to take steps, whether big or small. You will begin walking in the boldness and obedience that will bring you face-to-face with another human being. All you have to do then is open your mouth. You share and let the Holy Spirit shake. You see, there is no longer anything that can stand in the way of you daily walking out your God-given calling to go and make disciples.

Another way we could phrase the mandate of Matthew 28:18–20 is "The Great *Go*-mission." Everything about Christianity screams *Go!* Do you know what the word *Gospel* means? It means "Good News."

What are the first two letters of *Gospel*? *Go!*
What are the first two letters of *Good*? *Go!*
What are the first two letters of *God*? *Go!*

If heaven had traffic lights, they would be only one color. Everything about Christianity screams *Go!*

I meet people who are pressing into the prophetic who say, "If I get a word, then I will go." What they do not realize is, He already gave them a word and it was *Go!*

Riding the Roller Coaster

Many of our evangelistic efforts tend to be man-made ideas and structures, because the more in control you feel, the safer and less vulnerable you feel. There is the rub, however: Evangelism was never meant to be about us being in control.

In August 2019, we took a family trip to Disneyland. My daughter, Ruby, who was nine, was nervous about going on the Incredibles' roller coaster—the "Incredicoaster"—with me, but I knew if I could just get her to do it once, she would love it. She agreed, so sitting in our seats, imprisoned by the overhead rail, we prepared ourselves for what would befall us.

If you have ever ridden a roller coaster you know the drill. It slowly takes you to the highest point, suspending you over the edge, stuck in a moment of anticipation just long enough that the fear of what is to come can paralyze you before sending you free-falling at full throttle. And to think you are paying for the pleasure of this experience.

When you are at this most-elevated point just before the big drop, unless you are exceptionally brave, what do you do? Just like my Ruby, you hold on to the bar with all your might. This is because you want to try to maintain some semblance of control in order to bring some equilibrium to this feeling of being utterly out of control.

For those confident riders, however, it is a different story. What are the confident riders doing in this moment? Yes, they have their hands up in the air, hearts bursting with excitement at what is to come. They have done it before; they know exactly what to expect.

This is a perfect picture of evangelism, because evangelism, as I said earlier, is about our getting out of control so the Holy Spirit can get in control. The more out of control you are, the more in control He is.

When I train people to share the Gospel who have been silenced through fear, one thing many often will say is how alive it made them feel. Strangely enough, it is as if we are made for it.

I have seen many slick, outwardly eye-catching, theologically sound evangelism initiatives, but they are fruitless for the most part and devoid of power. Now, those pioneering them will say things like, "That is because it is such a hard ground we're plowing, brother," but the truth of it is there is no power because there is no partnership. When you have no Captain leading you so that you are the one in the driver's seat, you have to overcompensate for the lack of your partner's power.

James Bond Culture

This produces what I call the James Bond culture, where we have Christian operatives running around like secret agents for Jesus (*secret* being the operative word). They live out some kind of clandestine Christianity with plans to infiltrate the lives of their subjects via stealthy tactics over a lengthened period of time. Finding common ground, they bond over a mutual love of sports, music, food, wine or whatever it may be. Then when they feel they have earned enough equity with them, they play the Jesus card, unveiling their true identity, like Clark Kent confessing he is really Superman.

Set to this backdrop, it is hardly surprising we have evangelism techniques like Friendship Evangelism, which to me feels totally lacking in love and integrity. Become friends with someone with one agenda, but over time get them to drop their guard so you can reveal your true motivation, which was never really to be friends, but to lead them into relationship with Jesus. That is not evangelism; I would call that manipulation! If someone became my friend with the agenda of buttering me up enough to then lead me to Jesus, I would be deeply offended. It is all indicative of our lack of faith in the Gospel and in the Holy Spirit as our Captain leading the way.

I remember during my time as a student at London Bible College an extremely famous pop star came to perform a free concert for the students one evening. He was a Christian and was riding high on the winds of his secular chart success. At that time he was number one in the Billboard Top 100 charts in both the album and singles categories and seemed unstoppable.

He told us, "You may wonder why I haven't been open about my faith in Jesus. Bear with me, I have a plan. The higher I climb, the more favor I will have with people when I begin to speak out."

He maybe had one more successful album, then vanished into obscurity. He missed his chance.

Power Evangelism

You might be familiar with the term Power Evangelism, denoting a kind of evangelism that is personified by displays of God's power. This again is another example of how far removed we are from evangelism in partnership.

Many refer to evangelism in different tiers depending on the kind of approach, but to say a certain type of evangelism is the power kind and another is the friendship kind while another is the servant kind—and on and on with other kinds—shows how far we have drifted. *All* evangelism should be personified by power—providing it is in partnership with the Holy Spirit, because partnership equals power.

Maybe it is because of the lack of partnership that we have a lack of power, because we have dialed it down to doing something that costs us nothing, just some bare minimum to tick the evangelism box.

Safety Net Evangelism

We are hiding behind the safety nets of our churches, courses and other things, as opposed to stepping into the marketplace. That is where we would find the greatest safety net of all—the Gospel, held tight by the arms the Holy Spirit and a myriad of angels.

Deep down we have lost faith that the Gospel in itself is enough to transform a life. We have never stood naked before it, so we window-dress it instead.

We have dressed up church like a mannequin in a shop window hoping people will pass by and want to come in and take a look. We wait for people to be drawn in by our appealing programs, quality of coffee or childcare. We have retreated into the shadows of our own safe buildings, where we pray for revival and await the arrival of this mass exodus of lost people—who just do not come. The truth is we could fast and pray 24/7 for the next fifty years and the vast majority of our community would never cross the threshold of our church buildings.

Many churches are growing, but mostly through transfer growth, not through new converts. This leaves pastors fighting over a small percentage of church hoppers, all the while missing what is under their very noses—that there is a church just waiting to be established, and it is so big that all the churches in your city could not contain the size of the congregation. The future members are walking around your city every day, brushing shoulders with you in your supermarkets, sharing the water fountain at your gyms, dropping their kids off at your school gates, pumping gas opposite you, and walking their dogs up and down the suburban streets in your very own neighborhoods.

How are we going to see a move of God in our communities? It is not by waiting for a mass exodus of lost people to walk through our church doors. It will happen when the Church leaves the building in droves, being willing to have faith in the Gospel and trust in the Holy Spirit.

It will happen when we share and allow Him to shake.

‹‹ACTIV8››

I pray that you will accept the invitation that is being extended to you today. Begin to pedal, following your Captain on the daily adventure He has prepared in advance for you (see Ephesians 2:10), by putting one foot in front of the other. In Jesus' name, Amen.

SIX

GOOD NEWS IS NEVER INCONVENIENT

THE GOSPEL MEANS Good News, yet often as believers, when it comes to evangelism, we have this misplaced mindset that we are in some way bothering the people we approach.

Let's pretend that you owed the bank ten thousand dollars, and for ten years you were living under the shadow of that debt—red letters coming in the mail, calls from the bank, sleepless nights.

Now imagine I happen to have a check with your name written on it for ten thousand dollars, and for the past ten years I have been trying to find you. When I eventually find you and hand you the check, what do you think would be the first thing you would say to me? You would probably say something like, "I wish I had met you ten years ago," as that way you would not have had to live under the weight of such a crippling debt.

Jesus wrote us all a check metaphorically—not in ink, but in His blood—the most expensive check ever written. It has your name on it, along with those of every other human being who has accrued a debt through the wages of sin (see Romans 6:23). It is one check to clear the debt of all mankind's sins—past, present, future. Wow, what a thought—and although it was free for you, it cost Him everything. How is this not good news, rather than inconvenient news?

Get to the Point

Early into the conception of Jesus at the Door, I approached a man in his thirties and proceeded to walk him through the card. I had just finished point two, explaining the handle on the inside, when he looked me in the eye and said, "I want to let Him in."

"Eh, okay, great," I said, "let me just continue so you can know what it is all about. Lots of people pray—"

He snapped back, "I want to let Him in!"

Now, I was thinking that I had not even addressed the issue of sin, so if he accepted Jesus at this point would it even be legal? His enthusiasm was so zealous, however, that I abandoned the rest of the steps and prayed with him. His name was Michael and some months later I went on to baptize him in the sea, which had a ripple effect: His mom and other family members also came to the Lord and began attending our church. In some cases, the apples are so low-hanging, if you do not move out of the way they might just hit you on the head.

It just goes to show how good our Good News is.

The Dominance of a Godless Society

We need to stop living as though we are disadvantaged when it comes to being ambassadors of the Good News. If we do not view the Gospel through the correct lens, then we will be fooled into acting like an inconvenience to those around us. Think about the check analogy. What you are about to give them will change their lives.

It seems, though, as if the Church today has become conditioned to play by a secular rulebook. We listen to the voice of a godless society, the same voice that bullies believers into a corner, telling us when we can and cannot speak. This has resulted in safe-zone Christianity that causes us to miss the opportunities the Holy Spirit presents to us.

We allow a godless culture to dilute our fervor, to pour water on the embers of our enthusiasm, to demand that we move with the world's rhythm and dance to the beat of its drum. We, the Church, do not exist to sit tidily in a box on a shelf waiting for permission to come out on Sundays and special occasions. We live to make inroads where none exist. We set the standard for society to follow, not the other way around. The world does not ask our permission, nor does it care about offending the Church. In fact, the total opposite is true. The world shouts her agenda from the rooftops, forcefully proclaiming as if somehow speaking on behalf of society as a whole.

Jury Duty

We should by no means enter into a shouting match with the world, but at the same time we cannot allow ourselves to use the world's agenda as an excuse for not sharing the Gospel.

Sometime in 2017, while still living in Ireland, I was called for jury duty, so I drove the forty minutes to neighboring Antrim. Every day at a certain point an officer of the court would make his announcement over a loudspeaker in the room where we were gathered. He would either call your number or he would send you home.

I continued with this back-and-forth for a few days. The room felt like a cross between a library and a doctor's office—deathly silence and anticipation.

One afternoon while taking a bathroom break, I heard the Holy Spirit say, *Go back up there and tell them all about Me.*

My heart began to beat wildly.

Really, Lord?

I made my way back and pulled open the door to a sea of faces. More than a hundred people sat like some kind of human bingo, everyone on edge, wondering whose number was about to be called out.

I contemplated going back to my seat to plan my attack, but deep down I knew that if I did, I probably would not get up again. It is imperative when the Lord speaks or when we feel His tug on our hearts that we act immediately before the flesh can supersede the voice of the Spirit. Remember, the flesh is weak but the spirit is willing. So I walked boldly to the front and announced, "Excuse me, everyone, can I have your attention, please?"

Shocked at my voice piercing the silence, every head lifted instantaneously and every eye was on me.

"I have been given permission to share with you all this afternoon," is how the Holy Spirit formed the words as I opened my mouth. I thought, *Yeah, I like that.* The ultimate authority, the Judge above all judges, has given me permission. I thought it was very fitting, being in a courtroom and all.

I then held my cell phone aloft, akin to the moment Rafiki held up Simba in *The Lion King* proudly for all to see, and began to share the Gospel through Jesus at the Door. I was beginning to find my stride when I noticed two burly security guards conversing and pointing at me. They hurriedly made their way over to me. I knew I had only moments, so speeding up, I said, "Okay, now I am going to pray."

As I prayed, many in the room respectfully bowed their heads. The security guards allowed me to finish before cornering me and saying, "You cannot be doing this."

I sat back down, feeling happy that although I did not get to finish and as far as I knew no one got saved, I had obeyed my Lord. I confessed Him before men knowing that then He, too, would be confessing me before His Father and all the angels in heaven. That is always good enough for me, to know I have pleased His heart. It is important to be aware that we will not always see the fruit of our obedience in the moment.

The Bed You Make in Life

Some weeks later, back in the town of Coleraine where we lived, my wife dragged me along to a furniture shop to buy a new bed. My lack of enthusiasm was evident for all to see as I sat on the bed while my wife talked shop with the female sales assistant. As they were nearing the closure of the sale, the assistant began to look at me.

She walked over to where I was sitting and said, "I recognize you from somewhere."

Now, being a street evangelist who stood on the same street of my town for three years, I got that a lot. "Yeah, you probably know me from standing outside the town hall."

"No," she replied, "I don't live in Coleraine. I live in Antrim." Then her face lit up as she exclaimed, "You are the guy from jury duty!"

I got to walk her through Jesus at the Door, filling in the blanks that I never got to share in court, and she accepted Jesus right there in the furniture shop. Now, that is the kind of bed buying I like! It made me think of a quote I once read: "The bed we make in this life we sleep in forever."

I could have very easily been inconvenienced by my surroundings. Jury duty with a large crowd in a government building can certainly be intimidating. Shopping for a bed can be just shopping. But because I was not put off by my surroundings, I was ready, and a woman met Jesus because of it.

Scripture says this: "The earth is the LORD's, and everything in it" (1 Corinthians 10:26). It is time you start to own your zone. When you walk into a space, no matter how many people are there, no matter what they are doing, it becomes yours by right.

This is what the Lord tells you: "I promise you what I promised Moses: 'Wherever you set foot, you will be on land I have given you'" (Joshua 1:3).

Born of Water and Spirit

In 2015, my wife, Jaye, gave birth to our youngest daughter, Martha. At the time the whole scene felt very normal to me. It is only now as I write it that I can see just how special this encounter really was.

Jaye was lying on the bed, having contractions and in the throes of childbirth. The midwife was on one side of the bed like a boxing coach in her ear, in the corner between rounds confidently reassuring her that she could do this. I was on the other side of the bed nodding along to her rhetoric like one of the dogs you see on a car dashboard, feeling like a spare part, not sure exactly what I was meant to be doing. There are only so many times you can rub your wife's hand and say, "You're doing great, babe; not long to go now."

Not too dissimilar to a boxing match, there were lots of exciting moments I thought were going to amount to something, only to find it was just another anticlimax. So, producing my phone out of my pocket, I turned to the midwife and asked her, as I do almost every day to someone wherever I find myself.

"Yes, Scott, what is it?" she replied.

"Have you seen this picture before, and do you pray?" I asked.

Well, what happened next was better than any pain relief the midwife could have given Jaye. No gas and air, pethidine or epidural could have taken her mind off her final round of pregnancy more than what we were about to witness. I proceeded to walk the midwife down the nine steps to salvation. It was so beautiful. The Holy Spirit lit both her heart and that hospital room up with His presence like a Christmas tree. She got emotional as the Father's arms embraced her.

I often tell people how during this moment of exchange (sin for grace), it is like the world is on hold as you become locked inside this Kingdom moment. It was no different for us in this instance. It felt like someone had hit the pause button with precision timing just long enough for us to place Jesus' hand into the hand of our new sister to make an introduction, and then watch her fall headlong into His everlasting arms. It felt like the hosts of heaven were in that room with us as the tangible air of new life charged the atmosphere. Then we all resumed our focus, continuing in this theme excitedly to await the arrival of our new miracle of life.

Maybe as you read this you are thinking it was inappropriate or insensitive of me to evangelize while my wife was in labor, so let me draw your attention to those emotions. Feel those emotions, but then realize that because I took that opportunity, we were able to celebrate two new births that day.

As I have said so many times, if our midwife had not been a ripe apple or if she felt it was a bad time, she could have stopped at any moment. As people who share God's Good News, we have to stop giving excuses for the lost to stay lost. *Oh, this is a bad time. Oh, they might be offended.* Many Christians have twenty reasons why someone would not want Jesus—instead of two reasons why they would.

Might we ask instead, What if this *is* their appointed time of salvation? There is no inconvenient time for good news!

«ACTIV8»

Lord, I pray You will raise up this reader to be a pioneer and a trailblazer with a Kingdom focus to make inroads where none existed previously. In Jesus' name, Amen.

SEVEN

THE GOSPEL
IS A SLEDGEHAMMER

WHEN WE COME to the sixth prompt on the Jesus at the Door Equipping Card, our main objective is for the individual to have a revelation of the power of the cross and just how personal it is. We want people to feel that scandalous, outrageous grace that resulted in the Son of God pouring out His precious blood as an atoning sacrifice for the sins of you and me. He made it so easy for us: All we have to do is receive—receive the most expensive check ever written in the history of humanity.

It is important our recipients see the value of this sacrifice. Sometimes I will use analogies to really drive the point home, saying, "You could take the check, place it by your bedside and talk to it every night before you go to bed, but until you take it to the bank and make that exchange, your debt remains the same. The fact that you acknowledge that the check is real bears absolutely no difference to your predicament." Many people believe in the check, they talk to it every night before they go to sleep. Some wear it around their necks for good luck or hold it in their hands like beads, all the while expecting that in some way this will suffice.

When I speak from the card about this check being "signed in His blood," I often add these few words in order to accentuate the point: "Not with a pen."

These can be helpful things to say, but, ultimately, if you take away the Holy Spirit from Jesus at the Door, then you are left with an image of a man with a scribbled-out face and a few color-ful boxes on the back of a card. Yet when laced with the presence of God, it is simply explosive. His presence is the secret to our success. It is important to be mindful that you are not out there alone. While you are working on the outside of a person's heart, the Holy Spirit does an inside job.

Believing in the Power of God—or Not

In 2015 many Church leaders from different nations came to visit Coleraine, where God was pouring out His Spirit. I had the privi-lege of taking many of these leaders out onto the streets to give them firsthand experience with the Jesus at the Door Equipping Card. I would often get the same response afterward: "This is in-credible, but it wouldn't work in my city."

This frustrated me, as I knew the real reason we were seeing what we were seeing was due to the fact that the Gospel is "the power of God for salvation" (Romans 1:16 ESV). If those same leaders would step out into their communities, take God at His word and cradle the Gospel with the veneration it deserves, then they would see the same results.

The Gospel is a sledgehammer, and when you apply a sledge-hammer to a surface, something cracks.

Many believers hold the Gospel more like a feather. We are not tickling people's ears; we are smashing down the walls around their hearts, walls that have been built up brick by brick. As

2 Corinthians 10:4–5 puts it, we are removing "the strongholds of human reasoning... false arguments... [and] every proud obstacle that keeps people from knowing God." It is important we hold the Gospel with the honor and esteem it deserves.

God's Secret Army

We have a dream to mobilize every man, woman and child that bears the name of Christ, releasing them into the harvest fields of life. We call it awakening the Secret Army.

These are the covert Christians within the wider Church who feel sidelined when it comes to evangelism, people who feel they have nothing to offer in the area of soul winning and disciple making, people who have given up on themselves, people who have become so inactive that even the devil has given up on them, discounting them long ago.

I believe the Lord looks at those people, and He says, "They're My secret army," and when we can get them fully equipped and battle ready, everything will change. Only then could we have a move of God that the world has never seen before, where all believers go all in.

Here are true stories of some of these soldiers who were awakened to stand strong in the Lord's army.

Making the Devil Pay

I was training a great church in the Southeast, and as we always do after our Evangelism Made Easy breakout sessions on the streets, we gathered back for a time of feedback to share our glory stories.

It was clear Maria had a profound experience, because as soon as we all gathered around, she looked emotional, came up to me, hugged me and said, "Thank you."

She then began to share with the group how four months previously she had gone through the trauma of a stillbirth.

"Holding my lifeless baby in my arms," she said, "I told the devil he was going to pay."

Maria had never shared the Gospel with anyone before because she had a fear of being rejected, but now she and another lady hit the streets armed with nothing but the Gospel and the partnership of the Holy Spirit. Maria took the reins and approached her first ever person to share this life-transforming Good News. Very early into Maria reading the card, her listener made it clear that she was not really interested, so Maria thanked her and walked away.

She stood still, anxiously waiting for the rejection to hit her like a bullet train. She waited, and waited, and—nothing. No rejection came. It was as if the Lord had shielded her with His wings. Psalm 91:4 says: "He will cover you with his feathers. He will shelter you with his wings. His faithful promises are your armor and protection."

Maria then looked immediately for her next apple, except this time, due to her newfound protection, she decided to take an even greater leap of faith and approached two people.

I often tell people that whenever I get comfortable, I am looking to get uncomfortable. You will only grow when you place yourself in that uncomfortable space.

She began to walk them both down the nine steps to salvation and, lo and behold, they were both ripe apples, praying with her to accept Jesus as Lord.

As Maria shared this story with everyone, you could feel the faith rising. This once muzzled pussycat had become a roaring lioness (see Proverbs 28:1). With a newfound fire in her eyes, she told us that everything had changed, that this was the beginning of the rest of her life.

That is one more from the secret army awakened, enlisted and ready for service.

The Two Johns

As word grew about what God was doing through Jesus at the Door, my pastor agreed to let me travel one weekend a month. My first invitation was to a town in central England.

The pastor's vision was to invite me to train a couple of new believers in Jesus at the Door. Then we would spend four days going door to door around the community, and on the last day plant a church. That is exactly what we did.

Our first equipping day we had about 25 people in attendance. As I looked around the room, two individuals caught my eye because they looked so afraid. They were pasty-looking, knee-knocking, scared-of-their-own-shadow individuals. As I began teaching, I thought to myself, *Mental note, do not pair these two as partners when we hit the streets.*

But as we were pairing people up in order to send them out, I glanced over my shoulder and there standing together were the two men (I will just say they were both named John). Covertly, like two magnets being pulled together by their shared trepidation of what was to come, they had managed to find each other.

Nevertheless, counting the cost, into the fray they went, every step feeling like a thousand. Now, as fate would have it, they found themselves in the worst street in the whole community. Picture in hand, they approached a door and knocked.

The door opened and a large man with a four-inch scar down one side of his face thrust his commanding presence forward. I will call him Jimmy, and he was a gangster.

"What do you want?" he growled.

The two Johns replied shakily, "We would like to show you this picture, and ask, do you ever pray?"

Leaning forward, looking to the left and then quickly to the right, Jimmy snapped, "I have a reputation on this street. I cannot be seen talking to you out here. If you want to talk, you better come inside."

John and John expected this to be the rejection they had anticipated but were surprised to find Jimmy inviting them into his home, as though a divine hand had opened the heavens to cause this unlikely welcome.

Wanted for Kidnapping and Torture

Frozen in fear yet moving like lambs to the slaughter, they followed the path set before them. The door closed and Jimmy dropped a bombshell. "Before you say what you want to say, I better tell you both something. I have warrants out for my arrest for kidnap, torture and knife crime."

Silenced by Jimmy's confession, they huddled in closer to one another, their faces becoming whiter by the second. Jimmy told them to go and wait in the living room while he made them a cup of tea. (In England even gangsters offer the hospitality of a good cup of tea.)

The two Johns, as if broken from the spell by the sound of cutlery (which sounded like a knife, but was actually a teaspoon), glanced at each other. One of them, looking toward the front door, quietly yet dramatically whispered, "Let's make a run for it."

The other John, despite everything inside of him screaming, *Yes, run!*, replied, "No, I cannot run. I have to see it through, just once. I have to give God that."

So they stayed and awaited their fate. Jimmy returned and asked them exactly what they wanted. The latter John stepped up to the plate with hands trembling and head bowed low, eyes locked onto the multicolored card, and began to read it verbatim.

At the end he heard these words: "Yes, I would let Him in."

Dumbfounded, John paused to process what he had just heard. *Did I leave something out?* he wondered. *Did I present it incorrectly? Surely, it can't be that easy.* Despite his doubts, he walked Jimmy through the prayer to enable him to confess with his mouth what he now said he believed in his heart (see Romans 10:9).

They left him with a flyer about our local mission hall and hurriedly made an exit, trying to stay composed, but dancing on the inside as they made their way back to base bursting to relay their tale of triumph.

Their story reminds me of Reinhard Bonnke's autobiography, in which he recalls being a teenager and going onto the streets of Germany for the first time to share the Gospel. One man got saved. An elated Bonnke ran home to his dad and burst into the house exclaiming, "It works! It works!"

The Gospel worked for a fifteen-year-old German boy, it worked for the two Johns, and it will work for you. It is no respecter of persons. Just apply your B-O and G-O.

"Jesus Has Wiped Away My Past"

That is not the end of the story. The next day Jimmy woke up and started smoking his crack pipe. He had been bound in the grip of addiction for many years. This time, however, something was different. He soon realized that his narcotics were having absolutely no effect on him.

Perplexed, he exchanged the crack for booze, but he just vomited it right back up. His body was rejecting these toxic substances, as if the Lord had put a supernatural blocker in place to keep him from sinning.

Jimmy, now even more puzzled, suddenly had a revelation. He remembered the two pasty-looking, knee-knocking, scared-of-their-own-shadow individuals who came to his door with the Jesus picture. He remembered the two Johns. He began to smile as he remembered the prayer he prayed to accept Jesus.

At that moment, a car pulled up outside his house, blowing the horn. It was his gangster friends. Jimmy got into the car and off they went, but shortly into their journey they got pulled over by cops.

Turning to Jimmy's two accomplices, the officer asked them for identification, which they gave, and then it was Jimmy's turn. Now, remember, he had warrants out for his arrest, but he was a career criminal and well-versed in this kind of situation. As he was about to open his mouth to give false details, however, he heard a voice command, *Tell the truth.*

Stunned and in a quandary, Jimmy decided to tell the truth and await the outcome. The officer came back and spoke to his friends: "You can go. You can go." Then he got to Jimmy, who had already come to terms with his imminent arrest and pending incarceration, and he said, "You can go."

"I can go?"

"Yes, we have nothing on you," the officer replied.

Jimmy left his gangster friends immediately and hurriedly came to find us at our mission. He walked through the doors and exclaimed, "Jesus has wiped away my past!"

He then began to tell us firsthand this incredible series of events. As I stood with the pastors, we were awestruck by what we heard. It was a beautiful moment made only more beautiful by what happened next.

As Jimmy relayed his story, I looked to the side and caught the eye of John, who was making us all a brew (a cup of tea). Wow! Fewer than 24 hours previously, John was having a cup of tea in the home of this crazy, kidnapping, torturing gangster, not knowing if he would make it out with limbs intact. And now that guy was standing in our mission hall having his tea made by none other than John.

As I looked into John's eyes and saw his face light up like a Christmas tree, my heart melted. He could hardly contain his excitement as he listened to Jimmy's salvation story flowing like a river from his mouth. He was standing there as if thinking to himself, *I did that, because I stood my ground and did not run. I did that. That is my fruit.*

I knew in that moment that our ministry would be built upon finding the Johns in the Church. We call it awakening the Secret Army, those covert Christians who feel they have nothing to offer in the area of winning the lost. Our passion is to awaken this Secret Army that the devil will not see coming, as he already discounted them long ago, to rise up and win the world for Jesus.

The added layer to this beautiful tapestry is that three years earlier that same John had been admitted to a psychiatric hospital. He had lost his mind and spent his days in a padded cell. That was where Jesus met and rescued him. He was understandably still working through his own issues, but it shows that the Gospel is not dependent on how good we are; it is dependent on believing in the power of the blood of Jesus. The Lord will not force you. You have to move in steps of faith, but He has written the check. We just have to deliver it.

«ACTIV8»

I pray for you, if you have been holding the Gospel like a feather, that you will have a fresh perspective, that from now on you will see the Gospel as it really is. I pray that, holding it like a sledgehammer, you will begin to step out and apply it to the walls of hearts all around you. In Jesus' name, Amen.

EIGHT

STOP WAITING, HARVEST NOW!

I NEEDED SOMETHING that could move me from the sowing fields smoothly and succinctly into the reaping fields. I knew I was in possession of something that had been sprinkled with heavenly gold dust, but I still did not have a way to seal the deal, as it were. I needed a way to cross that invisible chasm that separates the person you are sharing with from not only hearing the truth, but actually meeting the Truth.

I had been seeing tremendous breakthrough in terms of both articulating the Gospel and in others' receptivity to it by using both the blue and red zones, but I desperately wanted to present the person with the invitation to accept Jesus. I needed what is now the yellow zone—the three points that reveal repentance.

Up until that point, more often than not, my strategy was to invite them to church, because then I knew they would encounter His presence through the time of worship and receive a great word from our pastor. In my head I was saying, *Get them to church. Get them to church.*

But the Holy Spirit was saying, *This is church. This is church.*

You see, the one person I am counting on to give them a life-changing encounter in the church building is the same person who can give them exactly that on the streets or in the marketplace—my evangelism partner, my Captain, the Holy Spirit. Everything you need is right there by your side.

Why I did not see that is the same reason you also have not—because we do not really trust Him, and we do not really trust Him because we do not really know Him. As I touched on previously, you can know Him in your secret place, but it is a whole other thing knowing Him in the harvest fields of life.

If you really knew Him, you would really trust Him, and it is the same with the Gospel. If we really believed the Gospel had the power to change a life in minutes, would we ever hold back from sharing it?

The Zacchaeus Moment

I refer to point seven on the card as the Zacchaeus moment. Let me explain.

In Luke 19:1–10 we read Dr. Luke's account of the tax collector who climbed a tree to see Jesus. The story of this vertically challenged man is so much more than the Sunday school song or childhood fable it has become. Did you know that when Jesus was passing through Jericho on His way to the cross to pay for the sins of the world, this meeting with Zacchaeus was the conclusion of His public ministry in Judea and Galilee? I believe there was a profound reason Jesus saved this little fellow until last. Let's look at the story in more detail, first from Zacchaeus's vantage point.

According to Dr. Luke's account, Zacchaeus was not in any obvious state of repentance, so why did he climb the tree? Here are my theories:

Number 1. He was an avid tree climber.

Number 2. He was on his 45-minute tax collector's lunch break and had some time to kill.

Number 3. There was something compellingly alluring about Jesus; he had never seen anyone like Him before.

I lean toward number three.

One day I had a vision of a school of fish swimming round and round in the deepest, darkest ocean. A big spotlight appeared suddenly, beaming brightly on the fish. They all instantaneously stopped, frozen in the moment, to look at the spotlight. The Holy Spirit showed me that it was because they had never seen anything like it before.

Like the fish, Zac was going round and round in the deepest, darkest ocean of life when all of a sudden, walking through the streets of Jericho that day, came a great big Spotlight—of the world.

Upon seeing it Zac did not care what he had to do, he was compelled to be close to that something he had never seen before. You may say, *Yes, that is because Zac was a filthy sinner, and not everyone will respond the same way.* Well, the Bible tells us we were all in the kingdom of darkness before God brought us into the Kingdom of His Son (see Colossians 1:13), so no one has a better or worse start than Zac.

It does not stop there. In Matthew 5:14 we read that we, too, you and I, are the light of the world. This means that when we walk through the streets of modern-day Jericho, we should light that place up like a beacon in the bay. We, too, should be that something they have never seen before.

Mistaken for Drug Dealers

While speaking in another city, I had some downtime on a Saturday, so I took my brother shopping. I purchased two hats but received no bag and no receipt. Walking out of the store past a security guard (there for shoplifters), I turned laughing to my brother and quipped, "We'll probably get arrested. They'll think we've stolen these hats."

After walking for a few minutes surrounded by hundreds of shoppers, out of the corner of my eye I saw a security guard bounding toward me. I thought immediately of the hats and began to feel guilty for something I had not even done.

The man got up in my face and said, "You look like someone who could get me a bit of sniff [cocaine]."

Taken aback and not sure if it was some kind of joke, I replied, "Nah, not us, mate. I'm a follower of Jesus."

I then realized it was not the coke that had drawn him toward us, it was God's light, so I pulled out my phone with our image on the case.

Before he walked off, I asked him, "Hey, as you're here, can I ask you something?"

I proceeded to walk him through Jesus at the Door. As I prayed for the guard, who had been on his lunch break and looking for some coke for a pick-me-up, he felt the love and power of the Holy Spirit washing over him. Right there standing in the main thoroughfare of this major shopping mall, he prayed out loud to open the door of his heart to Jesus.

What a beautiful day—he came looking for cocaine and left with Jesus. All because, like you, I am the light of the world.

An NBA Star Opens the Door of His Heart

My first time ever seeing a professional basketball game was quite an experience. I was invited by a friend of mine who is the chaplain of an NBA team to share the Gospel with the players in the gym before the game began.

We got there early, and he gave me a tour of the facilities. Within ten minutes of being there, as we passed by the court on our way to eat, a young man sitting on the bench on the court hollered over to me, "Hey, I like your jacket." He then beckoned me over to where he was sitting on the court.

My friend and I accepted his invite. Due to this being my first ever basketball game, I had absolutely no idea who my new friend was, only that he was overexcitedly complimenting me on my jacket. I realized quickly it was not the jacket drawing him, but it was because I am the light of the world. This player thought it was the jacket, but he was about to find out it was Jesus.

My only response was, "Hey, man, can I ask you a question?"

Pulling out my phone case, I asked, "Have you seen this picture before, and do you pray?"

I walked him down the steps by going through the card with him. I got to pray for him to feel Jesus, and did he ever. He paused with a startled look on his face, then looking at us both, he said, "That was powerful!"

I had a word of knowledge for him, which he said was accurate, so I was not surprised when he said that he believed Jesus was there.

Then, as I often do wherever I am, I acted out the last point to explain it better. I stood up on the court and began to demonstrate the turning of directions to make it more visual—facing one way, then the other. All of this was playing out courtside with many other players around having a pregame warmup.

As I did this, I noticed a little activity in the corner of my eye. Some people around us were beginning to take an interest in our talk, such as a television crew, announcer and press. Remaining focused in this Kingdom moment of divine appointment, the player said he would like to follow Jesus and accept Him, so I prayed with him to do so and we hugged.

As we walked away, my friend said under his breath, overcome with excitement, "He's the superstar player!"

When I got home, I followed up with him, the same way I do with anyone else I have led to Jesus. I found him on Instagram and sent him a private message. To my delight he responded to me within minutes with a private message thanking me for praying for him and giving him the word that I did.

The harvest is so plentiful that if Jesus, the Lord of the harvest, can trust His workers to be faithful, He will draw the people to you. He will do this as you shine out like a light in the midst of a crooked and twisted generation (see Philippians 2:15).

In order to shine, you have to know who you are and who He made you to be. Own it; take the basket off your head. "Arise, shine, for your light has come, and the glory of the LORD has risen upon you" (Isaiah 60:1 ESV).

You Can Never Judge by Appearances

Now let's look at Zacchaeus's story from Jesus' vantage point. We know wherever Jesus went, there were crowds of people, and what are people in the metaphor we have been using?

That is right, they are apples.

So here is Jesus, walking through the middle of a big apple orchard, and He decided to bypass all the other apples (the "low-hanging fruit"), in favor of the apple that seemed the most unlikely to fall. He went for a man who did not appear to be looking for God, a man who, from what we can decipher, seemed probably the least likely to respond, given that he was a notable sinner, chief tax collector and in no apparent state of repentance.

Looking him in the eye, Jesus uttered the shortest and most unorthodox evangelism technique I have ever heard: "Zacchaeus! . . . Quick, come down! I must be a guest in your home today" (Luke 19:5).

Then, just like the metaphorical apple, Zac came down the tree.

Jesus' first word to Zac says it all: *Quick!* There was an urgency; not everyone has tomorrow. Today is the day of salvation (see 2 Corinthians 6:2). So many in the Church today have lost their sense of urgency when it comes to sharing the Gospel.

What exactly was Jesus saying? In first-century Jewish culture, eating was a deeply intimate act, and to open your home was to open your heart. Zac knew exactly what was being demanded of him. Jesus did what He always does and goes straight to the heart of a matter.

He did not feel the need to mask or make excuses for His direct, urgent approach. He did not feel the need to engage Zac with small talk or beat around the bush in order to make conversation. He did not feel the need to ask Zac if he saw the game last night or comment on how dreary the Jericho skies were that particular afternoon. He did not need to create an atmosphere that was warm and fuzzy so He could then jump in.

No—He got straight to the point with assertiveness, immediacy and laser-focus, confronting this sinner with the power of the Good News of the Gospel.

You do not need the weather, or soccer, or basketball or anything else to help you find common ground when you have got the Holy Spirit. You do not need anything but Him. If you have nothing but the Holy Ghost and the Gospel, then you have everything.

The most fearful, cold, tense, unnatural situations I have ever been in soon become the most fearless, warm, peaceful and natural when the Holy Spirit commanded His presence and changed the atmosphere.

You do not need to hide behind anything. Right from the outset I like to be as authentic as I can be, letting people know why I am approaching them. People respect our up-front approach, as they know there is no ulterior motive.

Our Jesus at the Door image is based on Revelation 3:20: "I stand at the door and knock. If you hear my voice and open the door, I will come in, and we will share a meal together as friends."

This means we are saying the same thing today that Jesus said over two thousand years ago. He wants your heart!

Café de Jericho

How did Jesus know Zac's response was genuine?

Was it not all a little rushed and sudden? What if Zac were just getting caught up in the excitement and hype of the moment? How did Jesus know he was sincere?

Some people think the two minutes it takes to walk a person through Jesus at the Door is a little too quick. Looking at Jesus' method, I do not think we need to be concerned. Jesus proves that when words are laced together in the presence of almighty God it matters not how few they are.

Notice how Jesus did not say, "Zac, if you are interested, then tomorrow Peter will come back and take you to the Café de Jericho, where over the following twelve weeks, he will expound the Torah to you, giving you time to make sure this decision to follow Me is one you are really ready to undertake."

That sounds humorous but it would have been totally biblical. The Bible talks about counting the cost before you begin, making sure you have enough materials to finish building (see Luke 14:28).

But Jesus did not do that because that is called sowing, and you do not sow when it is time to reap. In the Church today we have a deeply seasoned sower's mentality instead of a relentless reaper's mentality, so we simply are not equipped to reap. We are happy to caress the apple and keep the apple company, yet we are not equipped to catch it.

Looking Through Heaven's Eyes

To address this, let's look at John 4:35. I often describe this as our bedrock Scripture. Jesus is talking to His disciples and references their order of doing things when it comes to the harvest.

Paraphrasing, He says, "You guys say it takes four months to bring someone over the line of faith (sowing), but there are people who are ready right now (reaping). You do not have to wait four months, four weeks or four days; you can have it right now!"

In order to obtain this harvest, there is a condition—you must open your eyes.

Were the disciples walking around with their eyes closed? No, Jesus was talking about their spiritual eyes, and just like many of us, their spiritual eyes were closed. You see, like the disciples, we count people out by the way they look, behave, dress, the company they keep or the language they use.

This is because we are looking through the wrong lens. We are looking through our earthly lens instead of through heaven's lens. Jesus is not swayed by an individual's outward appearance because the lens of heaven looks at the heart (see 1 Samuel 16:7).

If we adopt the same perspective, then everyone becomes a potential Zac—an apple that could fall today. With a Jesus-like perspective, possibilities are endless. No one is too hard to reach.

When I approach people, no matter who they are, I approach them thinking that today is their day until they tell me it isn't. Why? Because I know two things to be true:

1. Everyone is the apple of His eye, and
2. His desire is that none should perish.

Dirty or Shiny Apple

There are two ends of the spectrum we perceive when looking through our earthy lens:

1. The criminal, gang member, drug addict with a needle in his arm (the dirty apple).

2. The businessman CEO, earning a six-figure salary with a supermodel on his arm (the shiny apple).

One thing I have found these past number of years while working as a full-time evangelist is that those who are looking for God do not always look as though they are looking for God, be it the dirty apple or the shiny apple.

Jesus did only what He saw the Father doing (see John 5:19), and we must do only what we see the Spirit doing (see John 16:13). Stop counting people out and let Him worry about what apples do and do not fall. Only then will we be able to see the many who are like Zacchaeus, just waiting to be called down from the trees, like ripe apples waiting to be caught.

《ACTIV8》

If the Church becomes too preoccupied with busy schedules to allow the Holy Spirit to interrupt our days and guide us to approach the lost, then for those He can trust, He will interrupt our days by stirring the lost to come to us. May we be armed and ready to give an answer for the hope we have inside (see 1 Peter 3:15). In Jesus' name, Amen.

NINE

COME, HOLY SPIRIT

THE EIGHTH QUESTION is the most exciting question yet. It is the question where you have to prove to the person with whom you are talking that Jesus is, in fact, really there.

Do not panic—none of us can prove Jesus is really there. There is One who can, however: the One who reveals Jesus—the Holy Ghost (see John 15:26; 16:12–15)—who just happens to be your Captain. He is the One who is in front of you directing your course.

The previous point, point seven, asked, "If Jesus were here right now, would you let Him in?" It was the bridge to life, but now point eight is where we walk people across the bridge.

As God taught this to me, many questions ran through my mind. What if it did not hold? What if they do not feel anything? What if nothing happens? With all these concerns, I felt so out of my depth.

Without a doubt this point used to be my greatest weakness for the simple reason that at the time I did not know or trust the power that was available through partnership. It became my greatest strength very quickly, however, and still is to this day. In fact, it is my favorite part, the part where I often see grown men crying on the street.

Number-One Foot Soldier

I had led a young mum named Rose to the Lord, and she told me about her boyfriend, the father of her children. His name is Jack, and she wanted me to meet him.

I happened to see her meandering through town one afternoon with Jack. I approached them and we began talking. Jack immediately informed me that he would believe in aliens before he would believe in God. We continued this back-and-forth for a little while, and then Jack finished by saying if he knew God was really there, then he would be his number-one foot solider. But he was not prepared to leave his life of drugs to follow a God he did not believe existed.

One weekend as Rose was leaving for church, Jack became subdued and distant. His behavior was so erratic and out of character that she called me, upset and afraid.

I asked to meet Jack and, despite declining my invitation at first, he agreed after days of a persistent Rose pleading with him. Rose sat inside the café with her son while I tried to convince a very angry-looking Jack to come into the café with me to talk.

He kept saying, "I shouldn't be here," telling me that something was gripping his arm, and that it only got worse at the thought of going in there. It took a while, but he agreed eventually. As soon as we sat down, he looked me intently in the eyes with his nostrils flaring and his fists clenched. It was obvious there was some demonic activity at work. Jack is a big guy, and I did think he was going to hit me, as did Rose. Jesus was and is my defender, however, and I could feel the peace of the Lord upon me.

Jack was bound by a demonic spirit manifesting with a tight grip on his arm, the same thing Rose had experienced from the age of four until she got saved and set free.

I explained to Jack that if he made Jesus the Lord of his life, these things could have no power over him.

He said he did not really believe but reiterated his previous comment that if Jesus was real, he would become His number-one foot soldier.

I asked if I could pray and he said yes. I asked the Holy Spirit to let Jack feel Jesus in this moment, and he felt Him.

I then prayed and cast that devil off him. He was instantly set free. His whole countenance changed.

I then asked him if he now believed that Jesus was real. Although he was now much more open, he said he still needed something more to know for sure.

What else can I do? I thought. I had done everything I could think of, but I also knew Jack was so close to becoming Jesus' number-one foot soldier.

That was when it just came out of my mouth. Through my apple tree "We share, He shakes" revelation, the Lord had shown me how the Holy Spirit comes like a wind and shakes the apple trees, so I prayed, "Holy Spirit, come now like a wind. Let Jack feel Your tangible presence."

He came all right, like a wind. A beautiful, smooth, silky wind encircled the four of us as we sat in the middle of a downtown coffee shop. Jack's eyes were the size of saucers as he felt the breath of heaven upon his face.

I leaned over to Jack and asked, "Now do you believe?" He began to cry and, through hot tears, prayed with me to make Jesus the Lord of his life.

Even this was a battle. As Jack began to pray, their young son began to scream uncontrollably. Everyone in the café was staring at us. I had to stand on my authority and not allow this distraction to steal this precious Kingdom moment.

Within days he was on the streets with me learning how to become Jesus' number-one foot soldier. Jack went on to lead many to

Jesus in our town, and when I pioneered some small tent crusades in my community Jack was one of my main guys. He worked his heart out building and leading the charge with all the manual labor needed to make it all work.

Jesus at the Door works beautifully, giving the believer a framework that is built around giving the Holy Ghost breathing space. This is what makes it so powerful.

Less About You, More About Him

Praying for an individual to feel Jesus can often cause apprehension for the would-be evangelist. Some fear a lack of flowery words or a formulaic prayer might not harness enough of the Spirit's power to make their subject feel anything. Just know that when praying it is less about your prayer and more about His presence.

Again, remember your role in all of this. You are not the shaker; that is not your responsibility. You faithfully share and let Him shake. Be comforted knowing that, in your first few conversations, it may feel more as if the people you approach are doing the sharing and you are doing the shaking—from nerves! If you do, that is okay. The Holy Spirit will never let you down; His faithfulness reaches to the skies (see Psalm 36:5). He will also not abandon you as an orphan (see John 14:18).

Tips When Praying for Strangers

Remember the Holy Spirit does not need your hand. He can touch someone whether you do or not. If you are a tactile, touchy-feely person, then by all means place a hand on the person's shoulder; however, always ask permission first.

Do not close your eyes when praying. You want to see what the Holy Spirit is doing as you pray—and you want them to see

Jesus in your eyes. I prayed for a big Russian man once on a small plane. We were already way over the line of each other's personal space just by sitting next to each other on such a small plane. I shared Jesus at the Door with him. When I got to this section, everything inside of me was crying out, *Turn away, turn away,* but I kept my eyes locked on his, trusting the Holy Spirit to play His part. Needless to say, the man felt God's presence and opened the door of his heart right there and then.

As soon as you have prayed, ask the individual: "How did that feel?"

Draw it out: "Can you describe to me what you felt?" What you are doing in this moment is activating her faith, which is our whole objective.

The Bible says that there are two requirements for salvation: grace and faith (see Ephesians 2:8–9). Now, grace is as vast as an ocean—all you have to do is just jump right in—whereas faith is something that is required from the seeker. If we can activate their faith, they can then grab hold of the lifeline of faith and jump in deep into the ocean of grace.

Enough Faith to Receive

What if you pray and they do not feel anything?

I have found, after thousands upon thousands of people I have spoken to with this tool across the many continents, that when people do not feel anything it is because of two reasons:

- *The individuals are carrying such deep hurt that they simply refuse to drop their guard enough to feel God's love.* This is where a word of knowledge can act like a key to unlock that hurt.
- *They simply are not ready.*

Now, only God really knows a man's heart, so if you did not get a word of knowledge and you are unsure which category the individual falls under, just ask: "Do you have enough faith to believe He's here?" as it is by grace, but through faith that we are saved. Those who are ready but closed off through their deep wounding will reply yes, and those who are not ready will say no. That way, regardless of what they felt, if they have the faith to believe, they have the faith to receive.

Permission to Walk Away

While in training in Birmingham, England, once, a young man said, "I could never do evangelism."

A little puzzled I asked why.

He told me, "Because I would need to know every answer to every possible question they might throw at me." He was deadly serious, and this is not an isolated incident either. It is indicative of a sower's culture.

There are many, perhaps even you, who feel that without the ability to wrestle someone to the ground verbally in order to defend God, you are just not equipped. Hear this truth: You do not need to defend God; He can defend Himself. If that individual is not being drawn today, then no matter how much you wow him with your verbal prowess by regurgitating every apologetic book you have ever read or documentary you have ever watched, nothing you do will alter that fact that he is just not ready in that moment.

Sowers think they need all the answers, but as a reaper you do not need to know any answers to any questions. You are only looking for those who are being drawn. I am happy to tell you I am giving you permission to walk away. As I travel and train the Body of Christ, I find this brings a deep emancipation to the believers in attendance.

Now I am not saying never to entertain atheists. The Holy Spirit has the final word. He is in charge and trumps anything I say. But in my experience as a reaper, I would rather save you from the 45-minute debate that you will normally walk away from feeling as if your energy has been zapped. More importantly, you could have caught ripe apples in that time. But we need to be sensitive to the voice of the Spirit.

Filip the Atheist

One afternoon I stopped a young man named Filip. I tried to engage him in the opening question of Jesus at the Door, "Have you seen this picture before, and do you pray?"

He disengaged immediately, quipping, "I am an atheist. I only believe in what I can see. I do not believe in God."

Instead of my usual "Well, He believes in you" pat response, this particular day I skipped down to our penultimate point and asked, "Can you see the wind?"

He replied, "No, I can feel it."

I then asked him, "If you could feel Jesus right here, right now, would you then believe?"

He said, "Yes, maybe I would."

So I prayed. Within ten seconds this staunch, lifelong atheist looked at me so wide-eyed it looked as if his eyeballs might fall out, and he exclaimed, "My whole body is tingling, and I feel all dizzy."

Needless to say, he did not have a problem believing after that. Right there on the street, Filip prayed to give his life to Jesus, hugging me after he did so in a moment of heaven invading earth. That was Friday afternoon and by Sunday morning I was at his home picking him up for church, along with his girlfriend, Amelia, and their toddler.

Amelia pulled me to one side as they were getting in the car and said quietly, as if still in a state of shock, "Filip has never believed in God. When he came home and told me what happened I couldn't believe it."

She also accepted Christ, as did her family. The same morning at church he got offered a job and started the following day. After church he wrote this message on our New Believers group page:

> I am new in group and in church. Two days ago, I did not believe in God. When Scott stopped me in the street and started talking about God I laughed and said, "Don't talk bull——." He blessed me and I felt God inside me! Today I've come for the first time to church and God gave me a better job and gave me a beautiful, cheap room to rent.
>
> I believe God gave me a sign, and I want to repay Him for that. I need to learn a lot of new things; all of this is new to me. Can anyone help me to learn more?

Filip messaged me the day after his first shift at his new job saying, "Hey, bro, I've just finished work. It's hard, but with God I'm not too tired. God is amazing! I love Him! I love everyone!"

Both Filip and Amelia became part of our New Believers group and church community. I journeyed alongside them for the first year, watching them grow in the Lord.

That said, I rarely engage anybody past point number one if the answer was, "I don't believe in God." This is because, as a reaper, I am laser-focused, spending time to find my apples that are ready today to be caught, apples who may not have until tomorrow.

We Go Now or Not at All

In November 2019, while on a U.K. trip, I spoke at a church like none I had seen before. I had never come across a church compiled of so many scared people.

I spoke at their Sunday morning service. I then trained all who were willing to stay behind in the afternoon before we all descended onto the streets of their town.

I was so proud of that church. You see, many were not even planning on staying for the training. They had convinced themselves that they had to be elsewhere, anywhere but there. But many were so inspired that they stayed.

As we prepared to go, one lady disappeared into the bathroom. We found out she was in there weeping, as she was so afraid of going. There were others who were also shackled by that same level of fear. I could tell that the longer we tarried, the harder it would be to get them to leave at all, so we quickly got ready.

As we were doing so, a gentleman approached me with haste saying, "We need to go now. Otherwise we won't go!"

I felt so proud when I walked past the lady who had been crying in the bathroom, seeing her praying for someone on the street, hugging her, both happy and excited. It made me think of Ruby and the roller coaster that I talked about in chapter 4. They are my kind of heroes.

They all did incredibly well. The couple I partnered with led a couple of people to Jesus. The woman with us was not even going to go out, and it did not take long to see why. She was physically trembling as she spoke to a stranger. Yet within thirty minutes she went off by herself, not even needing our assistance.

Back at the debrief where we gathered to share our glory stories, the atmosphere was charged. It was like a room full of warriors who had returned from battle with their spoils of war. Weeks later I got pictures of the team out again doing the work of an evangelist (see 2 Timothy 4:5).

Are You a Psychic?

I have a dear friend, Jim, who refers to the way I hear from the Lord when using Jesus at the Door, as my "secret sauce." Truthfully, there is nothing secret about it.

When I first stepped out in this stuff I was vaguely aware of people who received words of knowledge when they prayed for others, although they were all pertaining to their recipients' sick bodies, bad backs and so on. I had never moved that way. I had never really moved in any way when it came to this kind of thing, so I did not really have a grid for it.

I love that kind of ignorance—not having a grid for something—as this meant I was a blank canvas ready for the Spirit's hand to apply His paintbrush to my life in any way He so pleased. I was just in a moment of "Help, Holy Spirit," and what happened next was breathtaking both to me and the people for whom I prayed.

When I first began walking people down step eight on our card, as I was praying for them to feel, the Holy Spirit would speak to me. This would become so strong, in fact, that it was as if He was interrupting my prayer to tell me something about an individual's life. I felt I had to stop my prayer mid-sentence, blurting out what I had just heard to this stranger on the street. Those moments were when I would most often see grown men crying on the street, with numerous people asking me, "Are you a psychic?"

I saw a level of power and breakthrough released through this gift, a whole manner of supernatural activity that blew my mind, so I sought the Lord evermore for it.

The Scriptures tell us we do not have what we want because we do not ask God for it (see James 4:2), so I went big. This prayer became my daily mantra: "Lord, give me the gift of the prophetic with lost people like none in this land, so that I may call out the secrets of their lives, that they may know You are real."

I guess my motives must have been right (see James 4:3) because the Lord honored my prayer, and I saw a rapid increase in the ability to hear the detailed personal secrets of a person's heart. In my first year I would get words of knowledge maybe for five percent of the people I prayed for, and by year two I was at 95 percent.

I Know Jesus, and He Knows You

As this gift grew, so did the magnitude of what I would hear. At the beginning it was small things like, "You're feeling depressed." This might sound like something to keep to yourself, but God can use it.

I trained a couple who were going on to plant a church in San Diego, California. As Kate, the wife, prayed for a young mum that she might feel the Holy Spirit, nothing happened.

Kate asked her, "Well, what did you feel?"

She stared blankly, then, sniggering almost mockingly with her friends, said, "I did not feel anything."

Kate panicked, turned to me and muttered under her breath, "What do you do now?"

In that moment the Spirit spoke to me and said, *She was in her room last night crying, as she feels so depressed.*

I spoke this out and the wide-eyed young mum did not look so smug anymore. In fact, she looked like a deer in the headlights.

She said the word of knowledge was true, so, turning to Kate, I said, "Now pray again."

She did, and after asking the girl a second time what she felt, the young mum announced, "My whole body feels on fire!"

Another time, I was training at one of my favorite churches, an amazing church in Nottingham called Trent Vineyard. During our time on the streets, I stopped a gang of young people ranging from 19 to 21 years of age. As I got to point eight, I began to pray for them, and the Holy Spirit revealed to me that one of the girls lost a sister when she was a baby.

I told her this in front of her friends and they all looked like they had seen a ghost. You could hear the gasps as they all looked at each other bewildered (we actually have it on video on our You-Tube channel).

One of the friends said, "Oh, my gosh, I have goose bumps."

When I gave the invitation, they all accepted Jesus. I then explained to them the same thing I tell everyone I give a word to: "Let me tell you why that happened. It is because I know Jesus, and He knows you."

The Key That Can Unlock a Heart

I describe words of knowledge by saying they are the key that can turn the lock to somebody's heart, releasing the secrets that have been hidden away there.

One afternoon a fifteen-year-old girl was in town with a few of her friends when I began sharing with her. She was being very nonchalant, being too cool for school, but as soon as I started praying the Lord spoke just one word to me: *mother.*

As soon as I told her, she burst into tears. She told me that just that afternoon, her mum had been diagnosed with cancer. She was so impacted and distressed, she called over her other school friends to tell them, and they were all equally amazed. One word from the mouth of God has the power to change everything.

Another time, I spoke to a man in his forties. As soon as I started praying that he would feel Jesus, the Lord spoke to me, saying, *He's got two kids. He separated from his wife, lost the kids and it's breaking his heart.*

I stopped praying and explained what the Lord had said. To ease his shock, I explained, "As with any relationship, Jesus talks back."

He said the word was true and went on to tell me that he gets his two kids twice a week, but it broke his heart when they left because he was not allowed to live with them.

Yet another time I went to Londonderry, Northern Ireland, with one of my new believers. I approached a couple in their mid-twenties. As I began to pray, the Holy Spirit said, *They have just lost a child.*

Now, I was nervous to deliver a word of this magnitude, but I knew if I was going to grow, then I needed to trust the Lord and His voice, so I gave the word. They were stunned, as it turned out that they had indeed lost their baby very recently. This word opened their hearts, and they both received Jesus.

One tip that can help you while using words of knowledge: If you get words of knowledge at any point while using Jesus at the Door, I advise sitting on those words until the moment when you pray for the people to feel Jesus. Then you can give your word of knowledge and pray for them accordingly. This will only enhance the moment of encounter, which you can then resolve by explaining the reality of repentance, providing the opportunity for them to arrive at the ultimate goal—the destination point of salvation.

ACITIV8

Lord, I thank You that when we give You room to move, You never disappoint. We may want to see Your Kingdom come in people's lives, but You want it more. Would You release a willingness for my brother or sister reading this to give up *all* control so that You can take *full* control? In Jesus' name, Amen.

TEN

MAKE FRIENDS, NOT CONVERTS

BEFORE WE LOOK practically at what goes into leading people to Jesus, it is imperative that you have first counted the cost and know what to do after they accept Him.

The beating heart behind Jesus at the Door has always been making disciples, not tallying convert numbers. For many Christians making disciples is nothing more than a buzz phrase, fridge magnet, bumper sticker or a nice prayer to pray at the end of a corporate prayer meeting. But how many are actually living out their faith on a regular basis?

Discipleship is not a program; it is a family. Like any family, it gets messy at times—but, oh, what a beautiful mess it is!

It does not cost you your life to preach the Gospel, but it costs you your life to make disciples. It will cost you emotionally, spiritually, physically and psychologically. I believe that is why the Church does such a poor job currently and generally of discipling converts.

I will not lie to you. Making disciples is often disappointing, as people will let you down, but how it draws the ear of heaven!

How Love Is Measured

It is a long road from the moment a person prays to invite Christ into the door of her heart to this newborn baby believer growing up into full maturity.

Billy Graham said that the five-percent effort to win people to Christ finishes when they pray, and the 95-percent effort to bring them into maturity as disciples within the Church begins. If we only do the five percent, we will only see five-percent results. How do we ensure we also do the 95 percent? The easiest answer to that is *love*.

The Holy Spirit once spoke to me: *Love can be measured by how much it cost you.* You see, love costs. No one and nothing exemplified that more than Jesus on the cross. It cost Him everything.

What was the object of His love? The world (see John 3:16). Love looks like God (see 1 John 4:8), love looks like cost, and love looks like others. Jesus said, "A new commandment I give to you, that you love one another: just as I have loved you, you also are to love one another" (John 13:34 ESV).

How did He love you? If we are really going to have a chance at making disciples, we have to love.

Counting the Cost, Receiving the Lost

During my three-year roller-coaster ride where Jesus at the Door saw hundreds of people pass from the streets to my house and church, the Holy Spirit told me, *If you count the cost,* then *I will give you the lost.*

It cannot be done from behind closed doors or from your armchair. We cannot compartmentalize it; it does not come all neat and tidy in a box with a ribbon on top. True discipleship is true love. And love is longsuffering.

I have been called out of bed to calm a drunk, violent ex-con. I have been robbed, threatened, slandered and almost arrested. But I would do it all again and more in a heartbeat.

Jesus never said to the Twelve at the end of each day: "You won't be able to get hold of Me between the hours of 5 p.m. and 9 a.m. Okay, lads, I will see you tomorrow. Keep your chins up. Stay out of trouble."

Now, I am not saying do not have boundaries, but I am saying you will have to open up your life. Think of it as extending your family.

I remember one Saturday afternoon when my wife and I took our kids to the beach, there was this great photograph taken of Johnny (who served 21 years for murder) next to my daughter Ruby, with big smiles and an ice cream in hand. That is discipleship. That is family.

Frustrated? Make Disciples

If you are a frustrated Christian reading this, it is because you are still hungry for more. Like a baby nursing at the mother's breast is innately aware there is more, her little head dances around looking to latch on to that more. That more for Christians is making disciples.

When I walked my firstborn daughter out of the hospital, I half imagined to be given a handbook or some kind of manual to show me what to do next. Then I realized there is no easy route, no quick fix. I just have to give my time, energy and love.

It is the same with making disciples. If you really love, you will gladly give the time and energy to watch this baby believer grow into maturity and blossom as you look on like a proud parent.

The Wisdom of Soul Winning

Did you ever hear of a midwife delivering a baby, then saying to it, "Okay, now you're on your own, kid"?

No, she hands baby to the mother, who then begins immediately to feed the child and model what life looks like to this new creation trying to understand its place in the world.

When a baby is being born, we do not let just anyone deliver it either. There is an experience, authority and wisdom in that field we rely on to ensure a safe delivery. That midwife had to work hard to become qualified in her field. We would not trust the birth of our child in the hands of just anyone. Well, the Lord feels the same way.

This is why He gave the Body of Christ the gift of the evangelist. The evangelist can help equip and model how this looks by example so that we can all become spiritual midwives.

As Proverbs 11:30 (NKJV) says: "He who wins souls is wise." There is wisdom in soul winning that people do not understand or appreciate, and therefore they often miss what is available.

We also read in James 1:5 (ESV): "If any of you lacks wisdom, let him ask God, who gives generously to all without reproach." What I believe the Lord has given me both in Jesus at the Door and the teaching in this book is a facet of wisdom that, when applied and put into practice, can bring a definitive new level of breakthrough.

Wrong Road and Right God

There are so many people on the wrong road believing in the right God, so the last thing we ask is: "Do you want to follow Him?"

Now, that is quite a bold question. I do not think that can be easily misconstrued. You see, it is one thing to pray a prayer to let

Jesus in, but another to change the trajectory of your life in order to follow Him. It is like falling in love—if you do not want it, then it will not happen.

I have had a number of people at this point in our process turn to me and say, "I am not ready for that," or, "I liked it all up until the last part."

I tell them, "Okay, I am not going to pray for you today to accept Jesus."

If I meet people who are not ripe apples in that moment and not ready to follow Jesus, I will gauge their level of openness. If they seemed open, I will point them to our New Believers group, church or to meet for a coffee to talk more and let the Holy Spirit do the rest, because when we leave He stays.

Put Down Your Gun

In March 2019, I was walking through Walmart with a friend looking for ripe apples in the town of Woodland where I live. As I walked along, I noticed a man whose name I later found out was Kyle. He was a big guy with lots of tattoos, standing in one of the aisles with his wife, who we found out was named Kellie. I was instantly drawn to him, so I approached him, engaging him in Jesus at the Door.

His response to me was, "Do I look like I need saving?"

He was being a little obnoxious and seemed very guarded, but did not shut me down completely, so I kept going. I proceeded to walk him down as many of the salvation steps as I could—which was not many—before he shut me down. But before leaving, I asked if I could add him on Facebook. The "We share, He shakes" principle works regardless of whether you are there in person or not—the Holy Ghost can cyber-shake, too. He agreed, so I added him there and then. I later found out he deleted me as soon as I walked away, but, hey, he could run from me but not from Jesus.

For obvious reasons, I passed that encounter off as two apples that were not ready to fall.

You can imagine my surprise two weeks later when my pastor messaged me to tell me about an email he had just received. In the email, Kyle's wife, Kellie, explained that they had met a man in Walmart, and they remembered he was from the Promise Church with the last name McNamara. She went on to say how it was imperative that they get ahold of me, so I reached out to Kellie immediately. It was Friday evening and by Sunday morning, both she and her son were sitting with me on the front row of church.

The time between when I met them in Walmart and when Kellie sent the email had been turbulent for their family. Kyle worked away in California, and every weekend he and Kellie would just drink and party while he was home until he flew out again on Sunday.

Despite their both having very good jobs, their lives were spiraling out of control. Kellie had previously been arrested for a double hit-and-run. One evening, Kyle drank too much and became enraged, and he hit his wife. The police were called, and things escalated quickly, culminating in a SWAT team being stationed outside their home. Kyle was shut away in the bedroom with the police on the phone trying to talk him down. Kyle sat cradling a gun, practicing how he was going to shoot the SWAT team one by one as they entered his home.

Then something happened. Kyle heard a voice telling him, *Put down your gun!* When he heard the voice, he became sober for about a minute and a half. It so pierced his soul and spirit that he obeyed the voice and walked out the front door. Once he was outside, he was blackout drunk again and fighting. He was tackled to the ground immediately by the many officers outside.

Hebrews 4:12 says, "The word of God is alive and powerful. It is sharper than the sharpest two-edged sword, cutting between

MAKE FRIENDS, NOT CONVERTS

soul and spirit." Landing himself in jail, Kyle was bailed out by his wife, who had a few conditions if the one-year-old marriage was to survive. One of those conditions was that Kyle talk to someone. Kyle's nickname growing up was "Robot," as he was so emotionless and shut off from others, but he agreed.

He told Kellie, "Okay, but there's only one person I will speak to—Scott."

Kellie replied, "Who's Scott?"

"The guy from Walmart."

And that is why I got the email.

Fast-forward to present day. Kyle and Kellie are fourteen months sober and have both been totally transformed by Jesus—so much so that when Kyle went back to California he led four of the five young men who worked for him to Jesus, using the Jesus at the Door card. He sent me pictures, showing proudly each new believer holding the card, all smiling from ear to ear.

One of these young men was Tyler, and when the Lord answered our prayer for Kyle to find a job closer to home, Tyler moved with him. Kyle was offered a job doing the same thing for more money with one extra day off a week, in—wait for it—Woodland, his hometown! Kyle and I baptized Tyler (along with others) in his bathtub, which was next door to the bedroom where Kyle was preparing to unload his revolver on the cops. It was such powerful redemption.

Tyler's girlfriend also opened the door of her heart to Jesus recently at our Revive New Believers group, shaking and in tears as the power of God fell upon her.

My friend and I baptized Kyle and Kellie during our Tent L.A. mission. They led ten people to Jesus through Jesus at the Door together as husband and wife.

Both Kyle and Kellie have become dear friends of ours, and our family loves them. They even came over for Christmas dinner.

Praying the Salvation Prayer

Once the individual acknowledges he wants to turn from the road he is on and follow Jesus, we then walk him through the prayer on the card.

The way I will often segue this is to explain: "If I were to come to your home and knock on your door, I wouldn't come in uninvited. Well, you said you believe Jesus is here right now at the door of your heart. You are just giving Him permission to come in." Then I lead the individual in a prayer that essentially matches the one on our card.

Some people have an issue with the concept of a "salvation prayer," and I understand why. Some have cheapened it to a kind of fast-food salvation—"Just pray this with me, then be on your way. Have a nice day." Remember, just to be clear, our desire is to make disciples, not to have people simply pray a prayer. Sorry to burst your bubble, but there are no magic formula salvation prayers that when prayed once will change a person's eternal destiny. When a prayer such as this is prayed in alignment with a repentant heart, however, that is when everything does change.

Why do I believe in a salvation prayer? Because I think it is key to help our new believer wrap words around this life-defining decision he or she is about to commit to, to form words that articulate the cry of his or her repentant heart. When the words of the mouth are fused together with the cry of the heart, then there is power. When I got married to my wife, Jaye, I did not just think the vows in my head. In a marriage ceremony there is a moment of declaration, and in that moment, something is released. I remember praying for a couple of young lads no older than twenty. After one of them prayed with me to accept Christ, I asked him how he felt.

He looked at me and said, "I feel like I just got married."

The apostle Paul said, "If you openly declare that Jesus is Lord and believe in your heart that God raised him from the dead, you will be saved" (Romans 10:9). We believe also that there is the power of life and death in the tongue (see Proverbs 18:21). Both of these verses show just how important it is for new believers to declare their faith aloud.

While words are important and it is tempting to judge the heart response by what you see in the outward response, sometimes you will not see on the surface what is going on in the heart. Do not discount people if they are not standing there weeping. Some of the people who have really gone the distance, becoming strong disciples in the Lord, came about from encounters such as these. You can never really know people's hearts; all you can do is present a clear, concise Gospel. What happens after that is between them and God in terms of their level of authenticity.

Making Disciples Is Making Friends

Okay, so the moment of salvation has just happened. You had the honor of leading an individual to Jesus as he prayed with you to make Him the Lord of his life. What comes next? Well, we do not wish him on his way saying, "Have a nice life! See you in heaven."

If you are going to make a disciple, it figures that you need to see that person again, so you just make a friend. That is it. Making disciples is just making friends—we have all been to school, so we all know how to make friends.

I never leave without getting a contact number or social media (Facebook or Instagram) details from a person I have led to the Lord. The vast majority of people who have gone this far will willingly give over their details without hesitation, providing that you do not make it weird.

Be matter-of-fact. I trained one older gentleman, and when he got to this part with the person he had led to the Lord, he said, "Eh, can I have your number? I mean, if you want to give it to me. I mean, only if you'd like to, then I'd like to have it." It became so weird and unnatural that I would not have given him my number. Just be natural; be yourself.

New converts have just said they want to turn from the road they are on without Jesus and change direction to follow Him, so you say, "Okay, now if you just give me your contact details, I want to help you take your first steps in this new direction."

The battle is always at its fiercest between the moment of conversion and the first step. This is when we have to exhaust our greatest energies. It is not enough to give them a church card and say, "See you on Sunday," for it can be a long week from when you met them until Sunday. Every day is another day you allow the devil to manipulate their circumstances to draw them further away.

Instead, I will message them and begin the fight (follow-up process) immediately, sending them YouTube links to watch, Bible verses, etc., doing anything and everything I can to help them to grow. I will also try to get a first-step meeting as soon as possible. If they do not reply to my text, I will call them.

A first-step meeting can look like anything you want it to. I normally meet people for a cup of tea or coffee and just touch base with them see how they have been since we first met. In a relaxed manner, I then dive into the reality of this decision they have made to follow Jesus, sharing how it is about a full surrender and giving Jesus the throne of their life. Together we look at Scriptures that will inspire them to want to give Jesus everything.

For most people, pursuing them will not put them off. On the contrary, it shows them how much you value them. Who would not want to be the center of someone's universe?

The Follow-Up Card

If our Equipping Card is there to make you more intentional about leading people to Jesus, then our Follow-Up Card is there to make you more intentional about making disciples.

MAKE FRIENDS, NOT CONVERTS

Our Follow-Up Card has proved very popular, and it makes this stage fluid and organic. While this card is not included with this book, you can order physical copies through the Jesus at the Door website (www.jesusatthedoor.com/shop). We also now have this feature available on our Jesus at the Door app, where you can electronically document the individual's name and number in the space provided, then hit "save." The Follow-Up card will be sent to the number of your new believer, who will receive the colorful card complete with the next steps to take on this journey.

If you prefer an electronic version over a physical copy, you can find the Jesus at the Door app in either Google Play or the Apple App Store. Once you download the app to your phone, open it, and you will see the option to subscribe in the upper right-hand corner. You can then sign in through the New Believers Info tab. As soon as you have an account on the app, you will be able to use the Follow-Up card feature (you can use the Equipping Card without an account).

Also, once you enter your new believer's information, her contact details will be saved simultaneously and automatically into your account under the New Believers contact info section. That allows you to access the list of your new believers whenever you need to so you can stay in touch with them and continue the discipleship process.

I Will Fight to the Very End

As an aspiring evangelist, you must go into this war with your eyes wide open. From the outset, you must be aware that making disciples, travailing for a transformed life, is a fight.

The devil is not going to roll over on his back and let you tickle his belly, so to speak. He *will* resist you with all he has when you come at him with an ardent agenda to see the souls of men set free. We must not be ignorant of the devil's schemes (see 2 Corinthians 2:11).

The devil will try every dirty trick in the book to keep people away from Jesus. We must show the same tenacity and resolve when fighting to bring them ever closer into their birthright as children of God.

How do we fight? Because our battle is not against flesh and blood (see Ephesians 6:12), we must use a different kind of weapon. Our geatest weapons are prayer and love (see 1 Corinthians 13:13). On your knees, therefore, bring the precious ones you have led to salvation faithfully (however briefly) to the Lord, before the throne of grace every single day and intercede for them. Then pursue them, love them—every text you send, Facebook message, phone call or coffee meeting is you fighting on their behalf to bring them one step closer. As partners with the Lord in this follow-up process, we must learn to fight for those who are the objects of His affection.

I reach out to all those I personally lead to Jesus regardless of the geographical restraints. If I am not able to follow up and disciple them myself, I will try my very best to get them connected to a church that can do that. For many, however, especially in the early days, I will keep in contact with them, pouring into them through whatever means available, be it Facebook, text or whatever.

If you have been a Christian for ten years or more, tell me: Does the devil still resist you in your walk with Jesus? I know you are telling me yes, so how much more do you think he will resist the ten-minute-old believer? The difference between these brand-new babies in the faith and you is that they do not know how to submit to God and resist the devil (see James 4:7). We have to show them how to stand firm in their new God-given authority.

In Matthew 11:12 (ESV), we read that "the kingdom of heaven has suffered violence, and the violent take it by force." One of the definitions of the word *violent* from the original Greek is a picture of someone in eager, energetic pursuit. I believe if we are to see the breakthrough we so desire to see in the lives of our friends, family, communities and nations, then we need to get a little more violent in this way. As enforcers of salvation, we need to be more energetic, approaching this war in a state of eager pursuit.

Some of us need to find our roar. Proverbs 28:1 does not say the righteous are as bold as a pussycat. No, we are as bold as lions!

Why does the Bible refer to believers as lions? Are we lions simply to sit in church every Sunday? If you think about a lion, it has no inhibitions. I mean you would not find a lion, standing in a zoo enclosure with everyone pointing at it, thinking, *Why are they all staring at me and pointing? I feel very self-conscious right now.* You see, a lion does not care what you think of it. It will proudly be a lion and not apologize for the way it acts. Maybe this is the reason we are referred to as lions: We are to be who we were created to be regardless of what anyone else thinks. A lion is built to stand strong no matter what comes against it. When it comes to the fight for the souls of men, there are a lot of times that lion side of you will come to the fore.

A Beautiful Mess

One summer afternoon in 2014, I approached a man named Rodney who was the brother of a notorious gangster in our community and had himself lived a colorful life. After our conversation it was clear that, although he had encountered the Spirit, he just was not in a place of repentance.

I gave him a church card, which had the details and address of our church, and said, "If you ever think more about this, reach out and connect with me." Never in a million years did I imagine what the Lord had planned.

A few days had passed since we had met. Sunday morning came, and Rodney was pondering a thought that had been planted in his mind: *Take out that church card from your jeans pocket and go to the church.* So that is exactly what he did.

He got dressed and called a taxi to take him to our church. At the end of the service, Rodney made his way to the altar. I met him there and got to lead him into the arms of Jesus. He immediately became part of our New Believers group family and church community, where he began to flourish. I went on to baptize Rodney in the sea, and his father also accepted Christ.

Rodney was the very first person in his particular New Believers group to come to me and say, "Scott, I think I'm ready to move on now to another group." He did not need the milk anymore; he was ready for the meat.

He became a regular fixture as one of our church parking lot attendees. It used to warm my heart driving in to church on a Sunday morning and seeing the radiant glow across Rodney's face as he directed people to their parking spaces. He carried out his job with such virtue he could have been a Secret Service agent preparing for the arrival of the president.

Six years have passed, and Rodney is still a regular fixture at church, still wearing that radiant glow, and still the first face many see as they arrive Sunday morning.

Ultimately, we plant and water, and the Lord gives the growth— but we must plant and water with everything within us. We must fight for these precious souls and do all we can to ensure they make it. Making disciples cannot be done at arm's length. It has got to get personal. It is going to get messy—but oh, what a beautiful mess it is. It is going to cost you—a lot—but the results are priceless.

Making Disciples from a Distance

People often ask me, "How do you follow up with someone that you lead to Jesus in a place where you do not live?"

This is a valid question. I share the Gospel and lead people to Jesus everywhere I go, so it happens often that I do not live in the place where we meet. This does not change anything.

I follow up exactly the same way: by getting their contact details and sending them our follow-up card. I then reach out and offer to help find them a church.

If I do not know anyone in that area, I will tell them to find a local Spirit-filled, Bible-believing church. If needed, I will help them find one through Google or word of mouth.

You probably know someone in the area where you are traveling, however, so see if that person is willing to help. This can be an excellent resource. While staying with some friends a four-hour drive away from where we live, I popped out to the grocery store. I shared the Gospel with a couple walking down the aisle. They both accepted Jesus and I got their phone number. Then, as soon as I got back to our friend's house, I connected them immediately with my friend via text. The following week I received a photo of both my friend and the woman I had met standing outside church together.

Another time I was in LAX (Los Angeles International Airport) and a lad in his twenties sat down next to me at the gate. I walked him through Jesus at the Door, and he accepted Christ, despite the fact that he had never heard the Gospel before. He told me he lived only twenty minutes away from a church where I had spoken, so I reached out to the pastor and asked him to meet my friend on Sunday. This young man went along, met the pastor and got plugged into their church family.

«ACTIV8»

Lord, I thank You that we are not alone in our quest to make disciples. You really are behind the scenes, weaving together a beautiful tapestry. I ask You right now for a revelation of the depth of Your involvement with us. Send that revelation to my brother or sister reading this. In Jesus' name, Amen.

ELEVEN

RAISING RELENTLESS REAPERS

WHEN JESUS SENT out the 72 (see Luke 10:1–16), He could have said anything. This was His Maximus Decimus Meridius–type speech (from *Gladiator*), His William Wallace call to arms (from *Braveheart*). It was His opportunity to give a rousing rhetoric to inspire His faithful followers to lay down their lives for what they believed to be true.

So what majestic mantra did Jesus verbalize in order to galvanize His band of merry men? He said, "The harvest is plentiful, but the workers are few" (verse 2 NIV).

Wait, is that it? I guess Jesus thought this was the most important piece of advice He could give the disciples in that moment, leading me to believe He would say the same thing to us today.

Scales Are Imbalanced

The Church of Jesus Christ is incredible at sowing, but less so when it comes to reaping. I believe a sowing mindset has established a firm footing over the years within the wider Church, leaving in its wake a culture of seasoned sowers, as opposed to those of relentless reapers.

The Kingdom of God, however, is made up of both sowing and reaping; one is not superior to the other (see 1 Corinthians 3:6–9). There does, however, need to be equilibrium. Yet in Christendom today it feels as if our evangelistic scales are culturally lopsided.

The Church is overweighed with sowing initiatives—food banks, debt counseling, healing ministries and discipleship courses; I have even seen free hugs. All of these are wonderful works that lead people (over time) into a deeper knowledge and awareness of the cross of Christ. We run courses, offer meals and give books we hope others will read, all the while desperately longing to give them the opportunity to enter a personal relationship with Jesus. We are not prepared or equipped for reaping, so—we sow.

We do not see this same tension in the farming community. Have you ever heard of a farmer who happily keeps sowing but never reaps? The law of the Kingdom mirrors the law of life—whatever we sow we will inevitably reap (see Galatians 6:7). Farmers do not plant a seed with little-to-no hope that they will one day reap a harvest. They have seen it so many times before, they know it is a foregone conclusion—it will happen!

We have lost the expectation for harvest because we do not see it anymore. With our reaper's mindset we have resigned ourselves to the fact that we must just keep sowing and leave the harvest to the very few "professional" evangelists.

Preach the Gospel at All Times

I remember a number of years ago there was a buzz phrase that seemed to permeate Church culture: "Preach the Gospel at all times. Use words if necessary." It is always attributed to St. Francis of Assisi, founder of the Franciscan Order, and is intended to say that proclaiming the Gospel by example is perhaps even more virtuous than actually proclaiming with voice. That quote always baffled me.

All we have to do is take a look outside our windows, turn on the television, scroll through social media or buy a local newspaper and it is apparent for all to see—using words is necessary! It has perhaps never been more necessary. Our dying, hurting world desperately needs to hear the life-changing message of the Gospel.

Besides, what about those who do not have time to observe our lives over a long period of time? What about those who perish before our Christ-stamped lives can reflect a close enough likeness to the goodness of Christ that they take notice?

Let's look to the Scriptures to see what they say. Paul states in Romans 10:14: "But how can they call on him to save them unless they believe in him? And how can they believe in him if they have never heard about him? And how can they hear about him unless someone tells them?" Then in 1 Corinthians 1:17, Paul also says: "Christ didn't send me to baptize, but to preach the Good News."

I decided to look deeper into the life of Francis and found he never actually said such a thing. In fact, he both lived and taught the complete opposite of "preaching" through actions alone. Yes, he said our lives should match our message, but we must still proclaim the message.

As it turns out, this phrase so often attributed to him, while it sounds so nice and so wise, is actually a lie, and an unbiblical lie at that.

This Little Light of Mine

I would like you to picture something for me if you will. Someone is drowning in the ocean and I come along in my lifeboat singing, "This little light of mine, I'm going to let it shine," wearing my best Christian, Jesus-loves-you smile. Would that save his life? Of course not; he would still be drowning. That would be about as useful as offering to pay for his swimming lessons or pointing him in the direction of a really good church. What he needs is for you to reach out your hand, take hold of him and drag him to safety.

Why do we think it is any different when it is concerning our neighbors, friends, family and strangers who surround us all day every day? If we are to become rescuers, we need to get up close and personal to the person or people we intend to rescue.

In John 6:44 Jesus clearly stipulates that no one can come into relationship with Him unless the Father draws him or her. The same Greek word translated *draw* in this verse is sometimes translated *drag*. It is used numerous times in Scripture, so to put it into context, let's look at a couple of these instances.

One time it is used is John 21:11 when Peter drags a net full of fish to land. It is used again in Acts 21:30 during a riot when a mob drags Paul out of the Temple. Now those fish obviously did not have a say in the destination to which they were heading, and Paul could not stop the force by which he was being dragged. In the same way, if the Lord was not dragging us to Him, we would not come at all. This is because the devil is on the other side displaying such a level of resistance, refusing to give up his hold of the children of God, that the Lord drags us forcefully from the clutches of darkness into His everlasting arms of freedom.

So what is the reason for this apparent cultural shift where we find ourselves surrounded by Christians who would much rather drip-feed the Gospel and play the long game? We have Church seats all around the world being kept warm by multitudes of spectators, but what happened to all the rescuers?

Jesus said, "I will make you fishers of men" (see Matthew 4:19). Where do fish live? They live in the water. People are drowning all around us, and we have a vast majority of Christians sitting on the shore fishing in the sand.

Prophetic Healing

The current flow of evangelism for a number of years in many streams has been moving in one particular direction, namely toward prophetic healing. There is nothing inherently wrong with this, providing that the Gospel is still preached and sinners are brought to repentance, but there is the rub. For a large percentage of enthusiasts, seeing a healing or hitting the mark with a word of knowledge has become the win. What was meant to be an introduction and invitation to the character and compassion of God (prophetic and healing) has become the crux and completion of the message.

In the fallout, some sort of proverbial bar has been set, projecting a standard of the way evangelism should be done.

The hesitancy here for me is, if this were the answer to our problems, then why do we have the vast majority of the Church still on the sidelines, looking on at those trailblazers, thinking, *I can't do what they do.* They sit there, continually reading more books and listening to more podcasts, hoping their anointing will jump out of the pages or seep through the airwaves to make them like the "professionals."

It seems to me most Christians see these prophetic, healing pioneers as though they are cut from a different cloth, birthed in celestial chambers, and sent down from heaven on chariots of fire. So the majority wants to give the vast minority a microphone and a stage on which they can tell their stories so they can score some sort of evangelism fix and live out their own evangelism yearnings through them.

All-Inclusive Gospel

We need an all-inclusive Gospel, one that everyone can own.

We need to lower the bar, telling the majority, "Hey, it doesn't matter if you've never heard a prophetic word before, or never prayed for people and seen them healed, because the Gospel is the power of God unto salvation. When you proclaim the Good

News in partnership with the Holy Spirit, everything changes." Releasing them with the Gospel, we move them directly from the sowing fields into the harvest fields, and as they go, they will grow.

If we can move them out from the bleachers in tandem with the Spirit, a natural overflow of this partnership will be their blooming in both the prophetic and healing.

If we are to see an unprecedented move of God in our time, if we are going to reap an end-time harvest such as the world has never seen, then we need more than the few "professionals" of the Church actively reaping in the harvest fields. As Jesus puts it, we need more workers (see Luke 10:2), or if I may paraphrase this, we need more rescuers!

We need to bring back a sense of urgency to the Gospel. I believe the apostle Paul understood this, and that is why he made statements like, "Today is the day of salvation" (2 Corinthians 6:2). He did not say next week or next month. The way he lived his life, like Jesus, reflected a man on a mission.

People Want an Introduction

This is a testimony from a woman in her late twenties. She wrote this on our New Believers group page. I wonder how many people just like this woman are out there wanting someone to introduce them to God. She wrote:

> I've never felt that I belonged anywhere. Consequently, I've been mixed up in things I shouldn't.
>
> Well, last year in February a friend and I met Scott up in the town. He explained a little about Jesus and what He was about but my friend, who was going through a hard time, brushed him off and gave him a hard time, shouting and swearing at him. I felt so embarrassed I walked away, still not really believing there was anything out there.

The last year has been more than rough. I've battled social services, barely getting to see my kids. I've had two suicide attempts in the last six months and have been at the lowest of lows, going back to living in a woman's refuge.

Today in the town I walked past a Chinese man singing about God. I could not understand a word he was saying apart from the word *Jesus*. I then stopped, looked up at the sky and found myself thinking, *I wonder if this is why I've never been at peace, because I've not taken the step and started to have faith.*

But straight after, I thought I was crazy. I went back to the shelter and put a post on Facebook about my experience, and a friend mailed me straightaway saying that this was God trying to reach through to me. It turns out that just two weeks previous she had become a Christian and had never been happier.

Then twenty minutes later I went back to the town center and I saw Scott standing there. I knew it had to be a sign; something had put me there at that time. I waited while he was chatting with someone else, then approached him and told what had happened since I met him one year ago. I asked if he could help me meet God.

He shared with me and prayed for me, and I opened the door of my heart to Jesus. I've never felt more at peace than I did then. He gave me details of the New Believers groups, so I will be there. Sorry for the long read, just wanted to share my story a bit and thank you all again for your kindness.

⟪ACTIV8⟫

Lord, I pray You would give all Your children an urgency for the Gospel so that we might move from being merely spectators into becoming rescuers. Awaken us to the multitudes who enter daily through the gates of hell. Bring balance to the scales and help us all bury the seasoned sower's mentality in favor of a relentless reaper's mindset. In Jesus' name, Amen.

TWELVE

TEMPORAL VS. ETERNAL

W HEN I FIRST began as a full-time street evangelist on staff for a local church, I would always pray for the sick first before sharing the Gospel. That would be my way in, my icebreaker, my equity earner. I did this because up to that point this was all I had seen modeled by others. I did not know there was another way.

Then when young people in my community began to die, be it through drug overdose, suicide, murder or just simply passing away in their sleep, I had a paradigm shift. I hit a wall. You could even call it a crisis of faith, not of my own faith but of the faith of others—those I desired to reach. It had become like an epidemic in our community.

I even officiated at my first funeral at that time. I was asked to do it by some of the rough, unchurched street urchin lads I had been reaching out to from a particular project. I was the closest they had to the things of God.

The Lord allowed this atmosphere of apprehension to provoke and quicken in me a sense of urgency for souls. Surrounded by the frailty of life, with the density of death looming over our city like a black cloud, something was changing in me. Whenever I looked into His eyes, I found myself looking through the gateway to eternity, reminded of my own salvation encounter. The catalyst for my own rescue came during a drug overdose as I stared down the gates of hell, face-to-face with my own impending godless eternity.

Sick Body vs. Sick Soul?

I then began to think of all the people I had prayed for, and even seen healed, who then walked away after they got their healing, never being given the chance to hear the message of the Gospel. How could I allow praying for the sick body of a stranger to supersede praying for her sick soul?

I decided from that moment on my leading leg would be the Gospel. I would no longer allow praying for a body that is temporal to take precedence over praying for a soul that is eternal.

So I stepped out one day, extremely nervous, feeling as if I was breaking some spiritual law. I approached a stranger and went straight for his soul.

"Excuse me, can I ask you a question?" Normally I would have followed up with, "If God could do any miracle in your life, what would it be?" But today I began, "Have you seen this picture before, and do you pray?" This was the first time I had tried the process that became Jesus at the Door. What happened next blew my mind.

Wowing vs. Wooing

I had a revelation. I realized I had been hiding behind healing the whole time because I did not really believe that the raw power of the Gospel could change the life of an individual all by itself in a matter of minutes. I also did not believe that going in so directly, broaching issues like sin and repentance, would present me with an invitation to see the Holy Spirit tangibly charge and change the atmosphere with His presence. Yet that is exactly what happened.

I realized, as the apostle Paul put it in Romans 1:16 (ESV), "the gospel . . . is the power of God for salvation." Like many, I had become focused on trying to wow people with a miracle, unaware that the Lord was waiting to woo them with the Gospel.

If we do not know the Gospel's power, we will feel the need to hide behind what we know. You can possess faith for a person's body to be healed yet still lack faith in the Gospel to heal his or her sick soul.

I have led many people to Jesus, and discipled many, and I can say that easily fewer than five percent of those accepted Jesus through a healing or miracle. It was not any less supernatural, however; they all came through the power of the Gospel as the Holy Spirit confirmed my words with a demonstration of His presence, power and love.

Hitting the Target Yet Missing the Mark

There was no stopping me after that first taste. I felt like an archer who had suddenly had the blindfold removed from his eyes. I could see exactly where I was aiming, and my arrows began to hit the target in ways I had only dreamed. I went from being a sowing evangelist to a reaping evangelist almost overnight.

Think of a target in archery. The gold section is the bull's-eye, earning the shooter maximum points. Enveloping the bull's-eye is the red ring, which earns the archer fewer points.

The healing culture that is prevalent in the Church today has done much good in terms of moving pew-filling Christians off their seats and giving them something to aim at. Countless spectators who had previously been sitting on the sidelines watching the other archers were now given a way to begin to play. Armed with their Kingdom arrows, enthralled to be standing shoulder to shoulder alongside the many archers they had spent so long looking up to, they began following in the footsteps of these professional shooters.

Many of these passionate rookies found they could, like their forerunners, hit the red outer ring. Now considering how far they had come, moving from doing nothing at all to being so close to the target was a monumental shift by anyone's standards. Enthralled by their success and growth, these new archers forgot about the gold bull's-eye section of the target altogether, focusing on just aiming for the red outer ring, making this their new bull's-eye.

This growth is praiseworthy for a time, but it seems most of the archers, both the old professionals and the new rookies, neglected to keep pressing on. No one mentioned the bull's-eye, as many of the older archers constantly missed this mark as well. Many were hitting the target yet missing the mark.

We have done an incredible job at teaching the Church to pray for the sick, and that is a wonderful thing, yet I fear we have failed in equipping her to share the Gospel.

Gangbanger Reduced to Tears

One time when I was training believers in California, my friend Brian "Head" Welch came along to an equipping day, which was quite surreal. Brian is such a beautiful man of God and one of the most purehearted men I have ever met. He is all about Jesus and carries himself with deep humility.

We sent the trainees out into the marketplace to put into practice what they had learned. Brian took me aside en route and said, "Scott, people think they're super cool in California, so it might not be the same as other places."

I reassured Brian it would be fine. That is the beauty of following the Captain each day—you never know what it will look like, but you know it is inconceivable that nothing will happen.

We split off into groups and, like a pack of lions hunting their prey, we began to prowl around the concrete jungle of an Orange County mall.

I took Brian under my wing, as he was keen to learn this tool. Not long into our time I noticed in the distance a few young men—trainees we had sent to the streets—looking extremely excited. They had seen Brian and me in the distance and were waving us over. When we got there, these lads were beside themselves with excitement.

Speaking with increased velocity, one of them relayed the story, saying, "We just stopped this dude named Max. He's a gang member, and he was walking with a cane due to his being shot six days ago in gangland activity. We prayed for his leg and he got healed. Look, he's walking off without his cane! It was off-the-hook amazing!"

By this juncture of the story, the storyteller was almost dancing with excitement.

"Wow! That is incredible," we said, as we celebrated this miracle.

I then looked him in the eye and asked, "Then what? Did you read the card?"

The wide eyes coupled with the long pause gave me the answer I feared, but I persisted, "Did you share the Gospel?"

He looked at me with all sincerity and said, "I don't do that. I just pray for healing."

He had apparently missed the "Gospel" part of our evangelism training because he was so convinced he had already hit the bull's-eye through his healing ministry. I told him to go and get Max and bring him back, so he went after him and brought him back. I then proceeded to walk Max down the nine steps to salvation. When we got to the Zacchaeus moment, asking, "If Jesus were here right now, would you let Him in?," he said yes.

I asked Brian to pray for him to feel Jesus, and that is what happened. There was Grammy award–winning rock star Brian praying for this gang member who had been shot six days previously and was now getting wrecked by the Holy Spirit, and in "super cool California" of all places.

Then it happened—the power of God that leads to salvation happened. This young gangbanger started crying. Taking the card from me, Brian then walked him through the prayer to accept Jesus. By now his crying had intensified emphatically so I embraced him. Then he really broke. He began weeping on my shoulder as his sins were washed away and his name was permanently etched in the Lamb's Book of Life. It was beautiful. It was Kingdom. It was the power of the Gospel. And it all happened in "super cool California."

Without meaning to, these young men had lamentably almost sent Max walking away fully healed, but straight to hell. Due to a lack of awareness, equipping and experience in presenting a full Gospel, what these young men were doing unintentionally was saying, "Excuse me. Hey, if you give me two minutes of your time, I can give you a more comfortable journey to hell."

You may say that is a little strong, but there are only two roads to walk in life—one leading to destruction (many find this path), and one leading to life (few find this path, see Matthew 7:13–14). In this instance we cannot hide behind the naive assumption that "he might have already been okay with God." He was a gangbanger, and the last I read, those who shoot people do not get a ticket to heaven.

This is so much of the current movement: We stop you, heal you and send you on your way. We have a large percentage of the wider Church waving their subjects goodbye after momentarily praying for some physical ailment, leaving legions of lost people continuing on the wide road straight to hell. And we call this success.

Sickness Over Salvation?

When Jesus was teaching at a house in Capernaum, four desperate men tore holes through the roof in order to lower their sick friend down to Jesus (see Mark 2:3–4). Now, there was no confusion for anyone as to what the friends wanted Jesus to do. This man was bedbound and could not move.

Yet Jesus, fully knowing the magnitude of the situation at hand, said, "My child, your sins are forgiven" (Mark 2:5).

You could hear the gears in the heads of those present, "Sins? Forgiven? Eh, what?"

It seems that in Jesus' eyes the sickness of this man's soul was more important than the sickness of his body. Then, after Jesus addressed some of the teachers of the religious law, He turned and said to the man, "Stand up, pick up your mat and go home!"

Jesus showed us His priority—sin over sickness. This makes perfect sense. After all, in establishing a culture where the catalyst for approaching somebody is healing, what becomes of those who have no need of physical healing? Are they shunned from our advances? Do they miss out? Does the fact that they are not physically sick disqualify them from hearing the Good News that ironically is the only cure for their terminally sick soul?

Not everyone has a sick body, but everyone's soul is in a state of sickness. Jesus said the sick need a doctor, referring to the spiritually sick who are in need of His healing touch of salvation (see Mark 2:17).

Be careful not to focus more on God's power to heal physical sickness than on His power to forgive spiritual sickness. Salvation is, and always will be, the greatest miracle of all.

«ACTIV8»

Lord, give us a correct perspective on healing in light of salvation. Help us never to forget the power of the Gospel that changed our own lives. The Gospel has never lost its power. In Jesus' name, Amen.

THIRTEEN

FROM RESCUED TO REVIVED

A TERRIBLE TEMPEST blows with wild waves crashing against the shore. The only challenger to the dominance of the darkness is a lighthouse—the Holy Spirit—whose light shines upon the many drowning souls.

Out of the darkness comes a ship, the Ship of Salvation. The Father is at the helm, steering His ship straight into the swell of the storm. Then He throws His Son, Jesus, into the throes of the screaming, wild waters like a lifeline. Whenever the perishing grab hold of the lifeline, they are saved immediately. The lifeboats then carry them to the safety of the shore.

I experience this dramatic scene every time I hit the streets. It is what I see when I look out into the world.

Notice in this scene, God is the only One doing the saving—we share, He shakes. But you and I still have a role, and not only in preaching the Gospel.

Once Jesus saves drowning souls from the storm-tossed waves, lifeboats carry them to shore. What are these lifeboats? How do we ensure they stay safe?

Jesus did not commission us to make converts; He commissioned us to make disciples. When I was hired as an evangelist, the strong desire was for me to lead one person a day to Jesus. I cried out for God to teach me how to reap, and He did, which meant I also needed to cry out to Him to teach me how to disciple.

For evangelism, God gave me Jesus at the Door; for discipleship, He gave me Revive.

Quotes from the Revived

Here are a few accounts of believers who were revived through one of our groups:

- "The Group was literally lifesaving. I was going to end my life. Everything was lost—my husband, my marriage, my children—but then I found the Lord. My life has changed so much since then. One of my kids is talking to me, and my family has changed toward me." —Colleen
- "Revive has been literally life-changing. I felt so lost in my life, but going to group helped me find my way again." —Jill
- "Through the Revive group, I've been able to have such a powerful interaction with the Holy Spirit that it has changed my life forever. I now no longer have anxiety because I learned to put Jesus first." —Bonnie

What Is Revive?

Revive is a Christian discipleship group with a twist, designed specifically for brand-new or not-yet believers. Our core values for Revive groups are simple, but essential. These are what keep us focused on what matters most—saving souls, discipling them, and sending them out to save even more souls. Our values are:

Rescue—Going out into the deep to rescue those souls who are drowning in the oceans of life.

Revive—This is the lifeboat taking them to the safety of the shores (the Revive group).

Release—The rescued become the rescuers. As we equip them in reaping-style evangelism, we send them back into the ocean.

Revive was birthed accidentally and organically in 2014 as a follow-up system to the large numbers of individuals who were accepting Jesus on the streets of Coleraine in Northern Ireland. I realized we needed something that could help these hungry new believers beyond weekly attendance in church—people who might not feel comfortable in a home group or cell group of mature Christians.

It was called GodSquad originally. We started with three individuals in our living room, meeting once a week on Thursday evening. Within three years we saw hundreds of people engage with our family of new believers, many of these making the transition into our wider church family on a Sunday morning.

For those needing to belong—it is *family*.

For those needing friendship—it is *community*.

For those who are afraid—it is a *sanctuary*.

It is about bringing people into their true identity as children of God, while at the same time making friends and having some fun. Revive is most importantly for teaching new believers how to develop this brand-new relationship with Jesus. It is a place where people can drop their guard, take off the masks and breathe in the atmosphere of God's love.

Revive is a place where people can be part of something that is real—a tight-knit group of people who will not only love you unconditionally for who you are, but help you find out who you really are.

There are many in this world who want to tell you who you are, but who did your Father in heaven create you to be? We invite people to come, be revived and find out who they really are as children of God.

Star of the Show

Our motto is "The Holy Spirit is the star of the show." This is the cornerstone to any successful Revive group. It can ironically also be the biggest stumbling block for leaders.

Just like in evangelism, the key to success is giving up *all* control so He can take *full* control. Remember the tandem bicycle analogy. We do not get off the bicycle here and neither does the Holy Spirit. We do discipleship the same way we do evangelism—in partnership.

It is all about partnership.

The goal is to make room for a continuation of the encounter the new (or not-yet) believer previously had with the Spirit. It is essential we do not get in the way of that holy moment the Lord has prepared.

As we mature in our Christian faith, one of our greatest challenges can be simply to maintain sole dependence on and childlike faith in the Holy Spirit. Nevertheless, that is what we want our disciples to see, so it is what we must model. After all, we want them connected to Jesus, not just connected to us.

A log can sit in a fire rubbing shoulders with another on-fire log but remain untouched by the flame. Once that log itself is ablaze, however, it is done; there is no going back. It will burn until it is gone.

Once it begins to burn, it begins to crackle. On-fire logs make noise, just as on-fire Christians do. They cannot help it. We need to take brand-new baby believers and put them into the fire among other burning believers. We need to do everything we can to create an environment where that log can catch fire, as only then can we know that they will forever burn.

What we see in our Revive groups is nothing short of Holy Spirit Pentecost fire. Pastors and other mature believers notice it immediately when they come to visit.

Umbilical Cords and Second Dates

As I have said before, when you encounter people on the street, you always want to get their contact information if at all possible. This is the only way to follow up with them, whether they received Jesus or not.

One great resource that we have found to be very helpful in keeping connected with those we meet is our private Facebook page for new converts, which acts as a forum for community and support. It is a place to feel valued, share your thoughts and feelings and receive spiritual daily bread. You have read a sampling of what some people post in some of the examples I have written in this book.

I believe one of the reasons our Facebook group for new believers has been so successful is because it is less intimidating for new believers to engage that way. It is a way for them to dip their toes into the water. In a sense, it serves as the umbilical cord to keep them alive in their newfound faith.

In addition to getting contact information from an individual after she has had her encounter with the Holy Spirit, we then invite her to take her next step by coming along to be part of our New Believers (Revive) family.

Think of your first encounter as a first date. Well, now we want to create an environment where that new convert can have a second date. When I first met Jaye, who later became my wife, I remember taking her on our first date. I brought my A-game, made all the right moves and showed her the very best side of me, as I really wanted there to be another date. I knew if she saw me again, I would have a greater chance to win her heart, which is exactly what happened (with a little help from the Lord, of course).

It is the same principle when seeking to disciple your new believer. In order to move her from the place of her first encounter (first date) to the next step of her second encounter (second date), you have to create an environment as soon as you can where the Lord can win her heart. Be intentional about this.

Order of Service

I want to make this as simple for you as possible. Just as God gave us steps to become relentless reapers, I believe He gave us steps to disciple all the new converts.

Revive New Believers groups usually meet in homes and work great there. The fact that you are willing to open up your home shows a transparency and warmth to the newcomer. I will say, however, we had to move our group to our church when it became impossible to fit everyone in our home anymore. This would be a great opportunity, however, to split and raise up new leaders from within the group.

Those who have a genuine love for people and a heart to see people saved and discipled make the best group leaders. The hosting homes tend to be the leaders' homes, but if this is not possible or viable you could find someone in your church—maybe a single person or elderly couple—who are happy to let you use their home.

Remember, the Holy Spirit is the star of the show, so the structures I am about to suggest are just that: a suggestion. It is merely the wineskin for God to put wine in, and if He starts moving, follow Him instead of some arbitrary order of service. This will help you, however, to have some idea of what we find to work well.

Snacks and Socializing

The first thirty minutes are a meet-and-greet time built around tea/coffee and snacks. We encourage everyone to make the effort and get to know one another, especially those who have been there a little while.

Introductions

We begin the formal gathering portion by welcoming everyone, highlighting the first-timers, who receive an extra-special welcome.

Then we go into our house rules, explaining that we aim to foster a culture of honor toward each other, so if someone is sharing, we show that person respect by not engaging in another conversation or talking over him or her. We cite Romans 12:10, which says: "Love each other with genuine affection, and take delight in honoring each other."

We share what we hope to achieve through our time together as the Revive new-believers family, which is primarily that by the end of the evening, all those in attendance feel one step closer to Jesus.

Enter His Gates with Thanksgiving

The Holy Spirit is the star, so we welcome Him by entering His gates with thanksgiving and His courts with praise (see Psalm 100:4). We do this by thanking Him through giving testimony of something He has done during the past week.

The goal in this is to foster a culture of thanksgiving but also to model accountability as people share openly with one another.

Some people will use it as an opportunity just to be heard, sharing their hurts or hang-ups, so we make it clear at the beginning that this time is not a time to air your prayer needs and struggles. We tell people that we will happily pray for those at the end; they just need to come and ask one of the leaders.

We continue to guide the group deeper into God's presence by building on the testimonies with a time of worship, sometimes with prayer or prophecy added. This is the time of the evening when we move out of the way to give the Holy Spirit room to move. We regularly see salvations, speaking in tongues and weeping as the fragrance of heaven is ushered in.

We begin by praying to give the Holy Spirit all control, then we have two or three songs, led by a worship leader on guitar ideally.

No matter who is in the room, be it a gang member or the queen of England, we encourage people not to tone down their worship but rather to give God the glory.

Baptisms

An important step for any new believer is to be baptized. When Philip, an evangelist in the early Church, led a man to Jesus, he asked to be baptized as soon as he found water (see Acts 8:36–38). My pastors have always encouraged me (or others I have raised up) to baptize our converts as part of the discipleship process.

I realize, however, that not all churches practice the same openness regarding baptisms. Some denominations prefer that only ordained ministers baptize new believers, so be sure to have a conversation with your pastor about your church's protocol before baptizing new converts.

We love baptisms. What the Lord does through the Revive group will send ripples of excitement and awakening throughout your church community. If you have baptisms as part of your larger Sunday service, it is a chance for everyone to celebrate together and give thanks to the Lord for the great things He has done. It will also raise the temperature of faith for evangelism among your congregation, spilling out into their lives also.

If your Revive group baptizes converts, then we recommend a bathtub, river, swimming pool or whatever works. Be creative, but most of all make it a celebration. You might want to host baptisms as part of your group's gatherings on a regular basis (see Matthew 28:19).

The Talk

Remember, this is a second date, not a Bible study. Resist the unction to wow them with your scholarly superiority and wisdom by expounding the hidden depths and mysteries of the Scriptures. Again, it is about letting the Holy Spirit do what He does best; give Him the room.

Do not talk too much. Our aim is not to have our new believers sit through a lengthy sermon. This can be difficult, as we often feel the need to talk whenever we feel nervous or anxious.

Play to your strengths. I feel the greatest thing we can do in these early days is to get people to fall in love with Jesus. Once that happens, everything else follows suit. This was one area that I excelled in (despite doing it by accident, as I did not know what to teach). If you were to meet the guys and girls I led to Jesus, there is a thread running through them all despite many being from crazy backgrounds: They all *love* Jesus. I just took the lid off my heart and let them all see what was inside.

Speaking practically, we recommend working through some sort of bite-size-chunked discipleship book. We use *Following Jesus* (Samuel Deuth, 2016) by Samuel Deuth and *ONE 2 ONE* (Every Nation Churches & Ministries, 2019) by Steve Murrell.

Choose an individual to pray to close out the meeting and thank God for the evening.

Network Partners Program

Ministries and individuals are implementing Revive groups as they learn about them. We plan on partnering with many more to see these flourish in communities all over the United States and beyond.

To help with this, Jesus at the Door created resources specifically to partner with pastors and leaders who want to implement, grow and develop a culture of evangelism in their church communities. We call it our Network Partners Program, and it gives us the opportunity to work in a deeper relationship with those leaders to help them in their efforts. Here are a couple of testimonies from leaders we have already worked with.

> Since moving to Texas, we have started a New Believers group that is very similar to the one that Scott had modeled for me. Jesus said to me that if I would create a net, He would fill it, and He has. In the last eight months we have water-baptized more than 170 people.
>
> Chris Donald, Lifestyle Christian University

> Jesus at the Door has not only led to easily more than a hundred salvations but has also driven us to be more obedient to Jesus in making disciples who will multiply. Over the past month we've been really intentional about the New Believers group. We already have seven guys in there who are on fire for Jesus, half of whom have been baptized in my bathtub, and new believers starting to disciple new believers!
>
> Jeff McClintic and Matt General

If you are a pastor who wants to partner with us, or if you are a leader who would like your pastor to partner with us, you can find details for our Network Partners Program on our website—www. jesusatthedoor.com. We would also love to hear from you or your pastor if you feel your church would benefit from inviting us out to run an Evangelism Made Easy day or weekend in your area.

Gang Hooligan Feels the Fire

I would be remiss to end without sharing a testimony of a life changed through one of our Revive groups.

Tears began to form in Janet's eyes shortly after I approached her and showed her the picture.

I started to walk her through our card when the Holy Spirit told me she was a broken woman, which I told her. She looked at me and said, "I'm sorry, I can't do this today." She ran off down the street, leaving me and her two kids stunned in silence. They then both excused themselves awkwardly and left also.

Compassion overwhelmed my heart, and I ran after Janet. I gave her a hug and asked if I could pray for her. She told me how her daughter had been murdered many years ago, and she had begun to feel that ache in her heart when I had stopped her (that day was also Mother's Day). Through tears, they all gave their hearts to Jesus.

Janet and her two children began attending our Revive group immediately, as well as church every Sunday morning. Janet had been telling me about her husband, Neil, and how he thought I was brainwashing them. Despite my numerous requests for her to arrange a meeting with Neil and me, she refused, telling me it was not a good idea.

Then one Thursday evening it seemed the Lord decreed this meeting would indeed take place. As I did every week, I went to collect the three of them from their house to take them to group (they had no car). That particular week I had a two-week-old new believer riding with me, sitting in the passenger seat. As the family exited the house, following directly behind them was Neil.

Standing on his doorstep, as if someone had flicked a switch, he became suddenly enraged like a wild animal, hurling a tirade of verbal abuse in our direction. To make it worse, all his advances were aimed at the young man sitting in the passenger seat of my car. What a nice introduction to Christianity!

Neil was shouting and swearing at him, even making threats to harm him. I opened my car door and shouted out to Neil, trying to talk him down, but he just ignored me as if I was not even there.

It was clearly demonic. Janet had to restrain Neil physically and force him back into the house to calm him down.

The following week, Neil invited me to his house as he wanted to apologize face-to-face. He later told me this was the first time in his life he had *ever* felt remorse for something he had done wrong. This is mind-blowing when you find out about his past, yet not so surprising when we read in John 16:8 how the Holy Spirit will convict the world of its sin.

As soon as I arrived at Neil's home, I could see he was agitated. I drank my tea, waiting for a gap in which to share with him.

"Hey, Neil, can I ask you something? Have you ever seen this picture before, and do you pray?"

With his arms out wide, barking back at me, he replied, "Do not come into my home and start preaching at me, lad! Football [soccer] is my church!"

Tail between my legs, I finished my tea and excused myself, telling Neil I had to leave. But first, I said, "Before I leave, is it okay if I pray for you?"

"Eh, yeah, if you want," Neil replied.

I prayed a safe prayer; you know, the kind that does not cost you too much. "Lord, bless Neil. Give him a great day. Thank You that You love him." It was that kind of prayer.

As I turned to leave, I felt prompted to invite him along to our group. In my head I was thinking, *Seriously, there is no way this guy's going to come, but okay.*

"I just want you to know, if you ever want to come along to our group, we'd love to have you there."

"I'll come," he said. "I'll come this evening."

In response to my surprised face, he continued, "I'll come, but only for my wife. I want to see what you all do there."

True to his word, that evening along came Neil with the rest of his family. Janet was sitting in the corner before we began, extremely nervous and not knowing what Neil might do.

I reassured her, saying, "Relax, the Lord is in control."

Neil arrived in a vest that ostentatiously exposed his army of tattoos, some of which bore the marks of the fascist groups he had been part of, such as the National Front (NF) and the English Defense League (EDL), who proudly bolster sayings such as "No black in the Union Jack."

With such a huge elephant in the room, the atmosphere was tense, but complemented by a pregnant presence of the Spirit of God, it was clear something was about to happen. None of us knew exactly what, however. We were at the mercy of His majesty.

We went around the room as the new people introduced themselves. When it came to Neil's turn, he proudly proclaimed, "I don't really believe in God. Football is my church. I am just here to support my wife." His comments left ripples of awkwardness in the air.

I tried to move on quickly. I remember feeling that night as though I was in the middle of something out of the book of Acts. Nineteen new believers were squished into our living room. There were no impressive lights, fancy music or smoke machines, but we had something better—the Holy Spirit and His raw fire.

At the tail end of the worship time, some folks began to pray. While everyone was praying, I noticed out the corner of my eye that Neil was wriggling about in his chair.

"Okay, what's going on?" he said, filling the silent air with his deep, defiant tone. This sudden outburst caused some curious people to open one eye, heads slightly lifting, wondering if they were allowed to look.

I asked Neil what he meant.

He continued, "For the past twenty minutes, my whole body has been on fire. When I try to fight it, it comes back stronger!"

Trying to compose my excitement, I asked Neil to stand up. My authoritative tone was a clear signal for everyone to engage fully in this supernatural moment as it was unfolding. I had recognized moments like these before, those out-of-my-depth moments when

Jesus steps in and says, "Thank you for trusting Me. I will take it from here."

Neil stood to his feet, and I called over a two-week-old believer (not the guy in my car; I think he was still shaking from his first experience with Neil). I put our Jesus at the Door Equipping Card into his hand and said, "Read it to him."

The baby Christian read the words, simply following the card, releasing the Gospel into the air. The Holy Spirit ensured every word landed right on target like an arrow of love into Neil's stony heart.

When Neil was given the invitation to follow Jesus, he accepted instantly and was led in a prayer. It was the most amazing moment to behold, a miracle for all to see, as Neil's whole countenance changed before our very eyes. He was born again in that moment! A stony-faced sinner transformed into a gentle-hearted brother.

Four days later Neil came to me on the street and said, "Teach me to do what you do." He had a thirst for more despite not knowing what that more was. He had such a hunger to lead others to Jesus that he spent every day of the next eighteen months by my side, giving of his days voluntarily to stand with me on the street doing the work of an evangelist.

Neil became very fruitful, and his special passion became leading people of other ethnicities to Jesus. This was an increased testament of the work the Lord was doing in his heart. You see, Neil's little brother had been killed by a drunk driver who was Asian. Ever since then his hatred toward Asians, Muslims and anyone who was not white only intensified. If Neil saw people of different races in a public place, he would often punch them, spit on them or verbally abuse them. But now all he wanted to do was love them. I took Neil to Nottingham on a trip with me and watched him lead a Muslim named Mohammad to Jesus in what was a very powerful encounter.

Neil was a man who had been diagnosed by psychiatrists as having an emotionally unstable personality disorder. He was once a football hooligan, heading up an organized football gang known as a firm whose sole purpose was to arrange rendezvous with other football firms and fight. Up to the point of Neil getting saved, he was still pulling the strings, orchestrating the fights between teams. Neil's past identity was a man who had a thirst for violence, an alcoholic and a womanizer. He even attempted suicide on two occasions. He narrowly escaped death when he tried to throw himself under a train and was just pulled to safety seconds before imminent death. At Neil's lowest point he ended up in a psychiatric hospital. He received no education after being blacklisted from most schools for burning down a school cafeteria. His reason for doing so was that he did not like the dinners.

One night after our Revive group finished, unbeknownst to us at the time, a young girl was about to walk home alone. Neil, being the total gentleman, sacrificed his own ride home to walk this girl back to her house to ensure she was safe. She lived in a notorious paramilitary-run project.

After Neil saw her safely into her home, he turned and walked away. As he did, a car pulled up and three men got out, circling Neil and asking who he was and where he was from. Before he could answer, they began to rain punches upon him. He ended up crouched down as they punched him.

Fights like this were commonplace in his past life, except with a different outcome, and because he got beaten up, he was embarrassed. It was over a week before he told me what had happened. I was brought to tears when he said, "I just could not hit them back. I have no hate in me anymore, only love."

At our church, where Neil and his family became part of our family, he is known as the man who likes to dance. Neil finds it hard to read the Bible due to his limited reading and writing abilities, but the way he can express his love for Jesus is to dance. So he dances—everywhere! He is just like David, who said he would become even more undignified than this, throwing off all restraints to dance unashamedly before his King (see 2 Samuel 6:14–22).

I went on to baptize five members of Neil's family—Neil, Janet, their son, their daughter and their daughter's boyfriend, who later became her husband after I married them at our church. Neil's baptism picture went viral on social media after some prominent leaders posted it. It is a beautiful picture of the face of freedom.

Neil has since completed a Bible college–certified evangelism course, and sometimes still travels with me all around the world to help equip believers.

----«ACTIV8»----

Lord, I pray You would give my brother or sister a desire not only to lead people to Jesus but to make disciples. May we lay down our lives just as He laid down His for us. In Jesus' name, Amen.

FOURTEEN

TOP THREE TIPS

CONGRATULATIONS, YOU HAVE made it through a lot of information. I hope this book will continue to be a resource to you as you go out into the marketplace to use what you have learned here.

I want to make this as simple for you as possible, removing any potential barriers between you and being effective for the Kingdom in reaching souls with the Gospel. Let's recap some practical tips that will help you most going forward. These can be your quick-find resource to help keep you laser-focused on finding the ripe fruit that is waiting to fall right into your hands.

Read the Card

Our number one piece of advice for the people we train in Jesus at the Door is to read the card. When people step out into the marketplace, they often hear a voice warring against them: *Do not read the card, do not read the card.*

People are nervous when doing a new thing. Their outreach is made even more difficult because they feel awkward not knowing the card by heart. They feel disingenuous, if they fail to look at the person the whole time. They will, consequently, approach the individual by reading the first point, but then drop the card and make up the rest. They dip in and out with a phrase or two from the card as they anxiously try to draw from their memory banks, instead of lifting the card to their eyes. This produces scenarios like this:

> Excuse me, have you ever taken a picture before? No, that's not right. . . . Let me try again. If you had a check in your backpack, would it be heavy? No, that's not it, either. . . . If Jesus was invisible like the wind, could you see Him?

I am exaggerating in order to overstress the point, but you get the idea. I promise you, the person you are speaking to will not be affected in the slightest if you never lift your head the whole time you are walking him down the nine steps to salvation. And the reason is this: It is not the power of your presentation that leads to salvation; it is the power of the Gospel.

Girls Bringing People to Tears

My first ministry trip to the United States from Ireland was with a wonderful church in Oklahoma. There was an eleven-year-old girl at my training. She was very nervous and would not look me in the eye.

When we got out among the people, however, this little, timid girl did exactly what I had taught her. She read off the card word for word, looking up three times, once at the end of every one of our sections on the card. The woman she was reading to burst into tears and gave her life to Jesus.

On a recent trip to Bend, Oregon, I took my nine-year-old daughter, Ruby, along with me. When it came to the breakout sessions, she went with the pastor and his team, while I took another group.

As soon as I got back, the pastor walked up to me wide-eyed and said, "Your daughter is incredible!"

It turned out that as they were walking through Walmart looking for whom to approach, Ruby pointed to a man, saying, "That one." She scurried off to introduce herself to the guy wearing a snapback with a pack of smokes hanging out of his pocket. She walked him through the card, and the guy started crying and prayed to accept Jesus. They even got a picture together, as the pastor was so impacted that he wanted to show me.

Stop Everyone

The second piece of advice is to stop everyone. First Chronicles 16:23 says: "Each day proclaim the good news that he saves."

We tell people to get a story a day and watch what happens—it will change everything. By "a story," I do not even mean a success story, just a person you approach each day to share with.

If you have ever shared the Gospel, prayed for the sick or tried to hear a word of knowledge for someone, I am sure at some point along the journey you have experienced at least one of these emotions: fear, trepidation or dread. If you are being totally honest, you have probably felt all three. Now, this does not (as some often think) discount you from being a fruitful evangelist. It also does not act as some kind of barometer for measuring your level of gifting as a potential soul winner. Jesus Himself said that the spirit is willing, but the flesh is weak (see Matthew 26:41). Not only is it weak, but our flesh wars with our spirit man (see Galatians 5:17), thus resisting us in areas such as these. That weak flesh needs to be silenced so that it can no longer be a dominant voice in our lives, stopping us from walking out our God-given calling as disciple makers.

How do we break free? Well, by proclaiming the Gospel! It is counterintuitive, I know, but the Gospel is "self"-destructive. The more you share it, the more your "self" will be destroyed.

The Chrysalis Conundrum

When a caterpillar goes through the chrysalis stage, it transforms from being a helpless, ground-dwelling larva to being a majestic, free-flying butterfly. But, for that to happen, the caterpillar has to wrestle its way out of the cocoon. It must fight to take hold of this newfound freedom. It does this by applying pressure.

Most would-be evangelists are like the proverbial butterfly— stuck in a cocoon. It is a cocoon made of fear, trepidation and dread. *What if someone asks me a question I can't answer? What if people reject me or laugh at me?* To escape that enclosure and be free, something has to give.

Before I take trainees out onto the streets, I am very candid and tell them, "When you come back, some of you will be exactly the way you were when you left. But for others, what you are about to do will change your life forever. You will forge your own evangelism wings and fly freely as the beautiful butterfly you were created to be. Which one you become is entirely dependent upon you."

I see big, buff men return to our feedback times after our breakout sessions, and I can tell by looking at them that they are still cocooned. Then I see small, sweet, shy girls who left cocooned and come back flying in with their newfound wings, no longer bound by restraint.

You must push through the discomfort. If you do not push through, you will remain encased in your cocoon. The way we push is by ignoring our flesh as it protests, *Do not do this; this is not who you are,* and by approaching as many people as you can. Every person you stop is like another hole punched through the wrapping of that cocoon.

When you are finished, regardless of what happened fruit-wise, you will discover a newfound freedom, possessing a pair of wings to fly freely for the rest of your life. As I tell people at our trainings, "Today is not necessarily about what happens to those you approach. It is about what happens to you." You see, you have your whole life to catch apples. If we can get you out of your cocoon, everything will change.

The Butterfly Effect

Picture a butterfly. Imagine that the left wing is evangelism, the right wing is discipleship, and the body is the Church.

When I visit a church to activate them in Jesus at the Door, our objective is to revive the church in both evangelism and discipleship. After we leave, however, many who intentionally press into what they learned only continue to flap the one wing—their evangelism wing. It is true the sustenance comes from the body, but if a butterfly only has one wing, then it will not be able to find food. No matter how much that wing flaps, the butterfly will never take off, and it will eventually die.

I celebrate every believer who steps out to preach the Gospel, and I celebrate even more every person who opens his heart to Jesus. We cannot forget the goal, however, which is growing God's Kingdom, and that requires us to follow through all the way to discipleship.

First Chronicles 16:23 says, "Each day proclaim the good news that he saves." We tell people to get a story a day and watch what happens—it will change everything. By a story, I do not even mean a success story. Just get a story of approaching a person each day to share the Gospel with them.

Do not stand around after every encounter evaluating how the conversation went, pulling it apart and dissecting every word. Just move immediately on to the next person. You will be amazed at how quickly the time goes and how you feel at the end of the experience.

Get Contact Details

Third and finally, get contact details. If you do not get their contact info, you cannot see them again. If you do not see them again, how can you make a disciple out of them? Phone numbers or social media are best. Avoid email.

«ACTIV8»

Lord, I bless my brother or sister who has read this book. Just as You shake when I share on the streets, would You blow upon this person's spirit, raising him or her up in Your power to become a relentless reaper for Your Kingdom? In Jesus' name, Amen.

Scott McNamara is founder of Jesus at the Door, the evangelism movement that is experiencing exponential growth due to its all-inclusive, Gospel-centered approach, providing everyday believers with a practical, yet powerful way to lead people to Jesus.

Scott's desire is to awaken the sleeping giant of evangelism—the wider Church—and remind her that the Great Commission was not given to evangelists, but to disciples.

God has placed His favor on Scott and entrusted him with the office of an evangelist. He travels the world, equipping the Body of Christ to bury an exclusively sower's mentality in favor of that of a relentless reaper.

Scott was featured in the Christian documentary *Finger of God 2*, alongside Christian rock star and Korn guitarist Brian "Head" Welch.

Scott is married to Jaye and together they have four beautiful children—Sienna (thirteen), Ruby (ten), Elijah (seven) and Martha (five).